Junior Atlas
of the world

Chez Picthall & Dominic Zwemmer

picthall and gunzi

picthall and gunzi

Created and produced by
Picthall & Gunzi Limited
21A Widmore Road Bromley BR1 1RW
United Kingdom

Copyright © 2011 Picthall and Gunzi Limited

Digital Cartography:
Encompass Graphics Ltd, U.K.
Cartographic Consultant: Roger Bullen

Original concept: Chez Picthall
Editorial: Christiane Gunzi
Art Direction and design: Dominic Zwemmer
Picture Research: Dominic Zwemmer
and Katy Rayner

Indexer: Marie Lorimer
Production: Toby Reynolds and
Alastair Gourlay

ISBN 978 1 906572 92 1

Reproduction by Colourscan,
Printed and bound in Malaysia

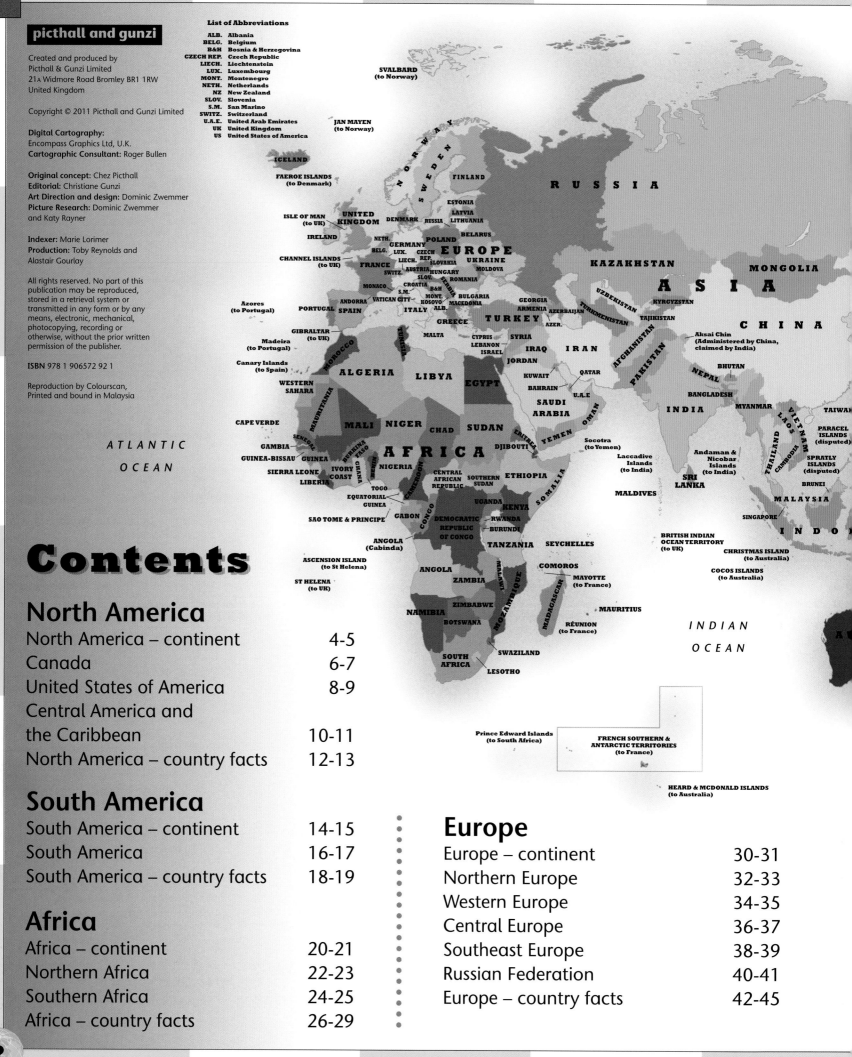

List of Abbreviations

ALB.	Albania
BELG.	Belgium
B&H	Bosnia & Herzegovina
CZECH REP.	Czech Republic
LIECH.	Liechtenstein
LUX.	Luxembourg
MONT.	Montenegro
NETH.	Netherlands
NZ	New Zealand
SLOV.	Slovenia
S.M.	San Marino
SWITZ.	Switzerland
U.A.E.	United Arab Emirates
UK	United Kingdom
US	United States of America

Contents

North America

South America

Africa

Europe

Asia

Australasia and Oceania

Arctic and Antarctica

North America

This is the third-largest continent in the world, with 23 countries. It stretches from Greenland, where it is freezing, to the Caribbean, where it is hot. The first people came here from Asia 20,000 years ago. About 500 years ago people from Europe, Africa and Asia started to arrive, with their new languages and religions.

ARCTIC OCEAN

UNITED STATES OF AMERICA (Alaska)

C   A

Biggest country

Canada is North America's biggest country. Its border with the United States is the longest in the world. The huge Niagara Falls form part of this border. This enormous waterfall is in Canada and in the United States too!

Biggest city

PACIFIC OCEAN

More people live in Mexico City than any other city in North America. There are over 20 million people in this lively place!

U.S.A. (Hawaii)

ABOUT NORTH AMERICA

NUMBER OF COUNTRIES	23
SIZE	World's 3rd-largest continent
TOTAL AREA	24,709,000 sq kilometres
POPULATION	528,720,588 million people
BIGGEST COUNTRY	Canada – 9,984,670 square kilometres
SMALLEST COUNTRY	St Kitts and Nevis – total area 261 square kilometres
BIGGEST CITY	Mexico City, Mexico

THE WOW!

The border between Mexico and The United States of America is the busiest border in the world! More than 250 million people cross this border every year.

FACTOR

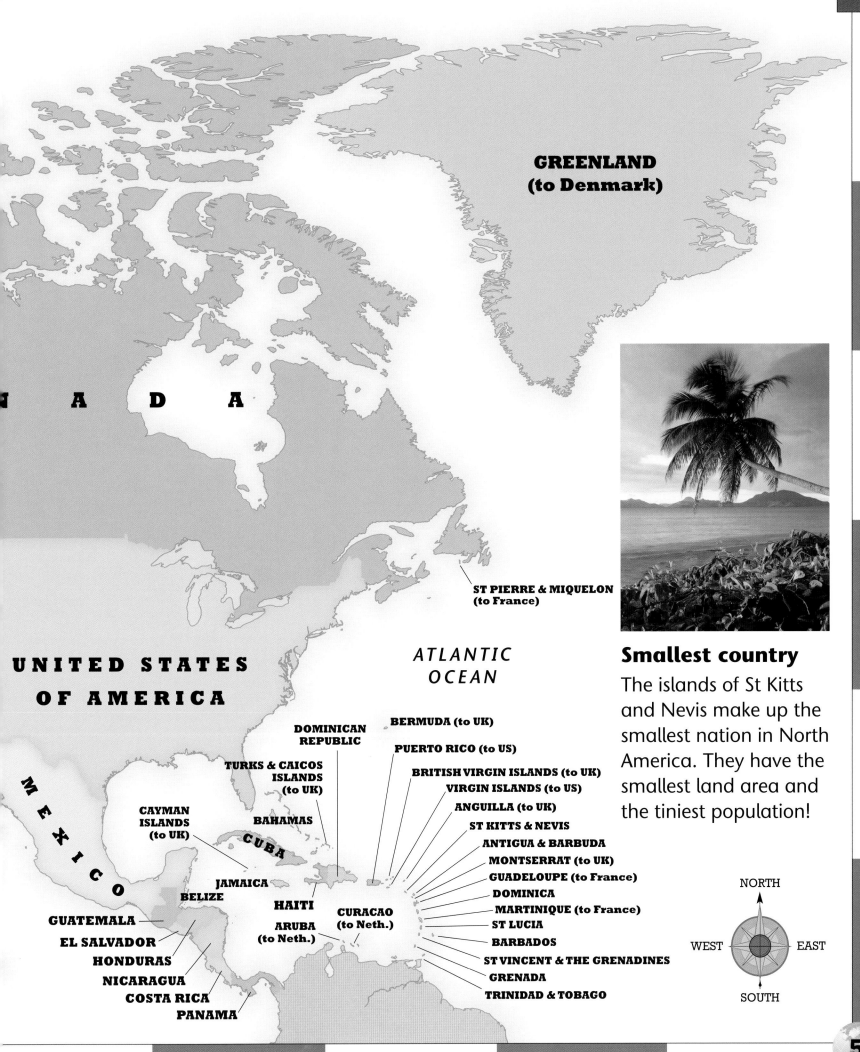

GREENLAND (to Denmark)

C A N A D A

ST PIERRE & MIQUELON (to France)

UNITED STATES OF AMERICA

ATLANTIC OCEAN

M E X I C O

CAYMAN ISLANDS (to UK)

BAHAMAS

C U B A

JAMAICA

BELIZE

GUATEMALA

EL SALVADOR

HONDURAS

NICARAGUA

COSTA RICA

PANAMA

HAITI

ARUBA (to Neth.)

CURACAO (to Neth.)

DOMINICAN REPUBLIC

TURKS & CAICOS ISLANDS (to UK)

BERMUDA (to UK)

PUERTO RICO (to US)

BRITISH VIRGIN ISLANDS (to UK)

VIRGIN ISLANDS (to US)

ANGUILLA (to UK)

ST KITTS & NEVIS

ANTIGUA & BARBUDA

MONTSERRAT (to UK)

GUADELOUPE (to France)

DOMINICA

MARTINIQUE (to France)

ST LUCIA

BARBADOS

ST VINCENT & THE GRENADINES

GRENADA

TRINIDAD & TOBAGO

Smallest country

The islands of St Kitts and Nevis make up the smallest nation in North America. They have the smallest land area and the tiniest population!

NORTH

WEST   EAST

SOUTH

Canada

Canada is the second-biggest country in the world, after Russia. A lot of Canada is covered by forests and grasslands, and thousands of lakes and rivers. The north gets very cold and snowy, and the land freezes in winter, so hardly any people live there. Mining, paper-making and fishing are important industries for Canada.

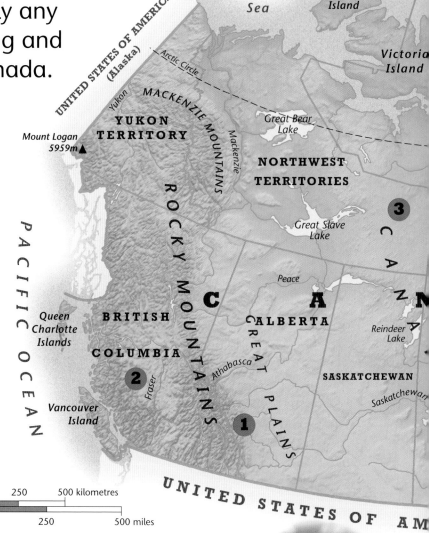

1 Canoeing in Canada

An exciting way to explore many of the 42 national parks in Canada is to travel on the lakes and rivers by kayak or canoe.

2 Mountain lion

The mountain lion is also known as a puma and a cougar. These cats are shy and prefer to live in wild places like the Rocky Mountains.

3 Blue jay

These clever birds are related to magpies and crows. They can copy the sounds of other birds, and human voices too!

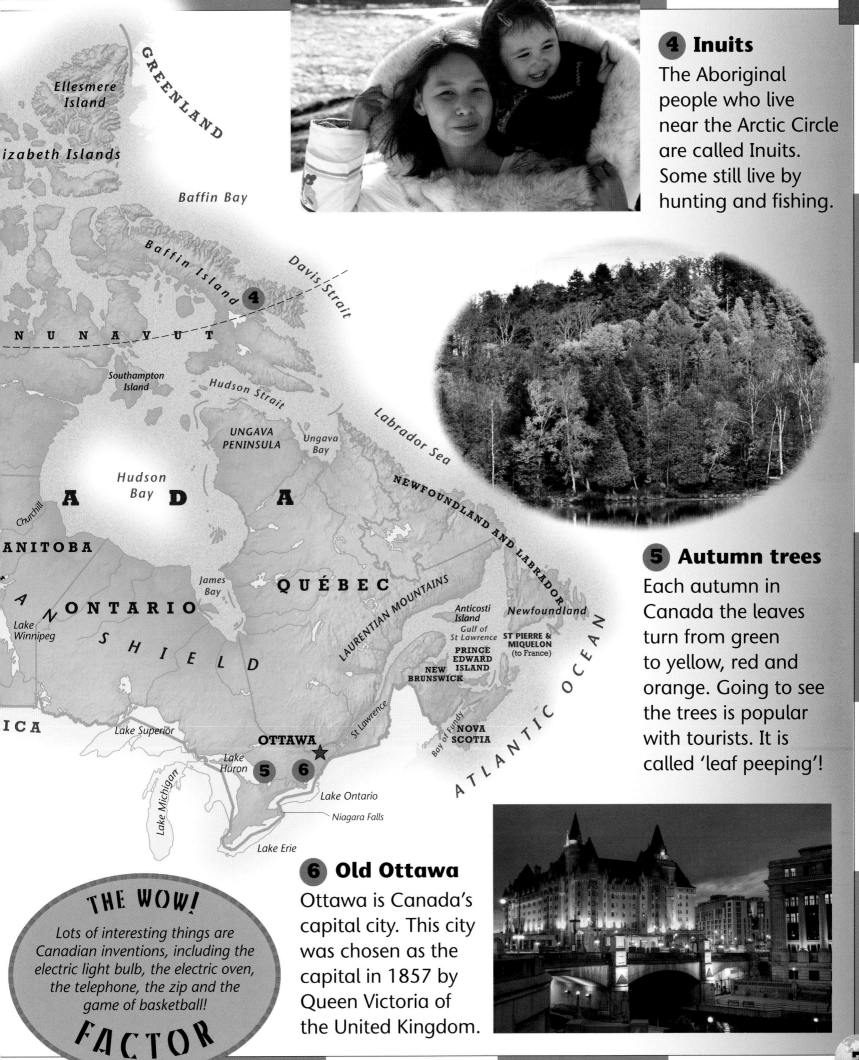

4 Inuits

The Aboriginal people who live near the Arctic Circle are called Inuits. Some still live by hunting and fishing.

5 Autumn trees

Each autumn in Canada the leaves turn from green to yellow, red and orange. Going to see the trees is popular with tourists. It is called 'leaf peeping'!

6 Old Ottawa

Ottawa is Canada's capital city. This city was chosen as the capital in 1857 by Queen Victoria of the United Kingdom.

THE WOW!

Lots of interesting things are Canadian inventions, including the electric light bulb, the electric oven, the telephone, the zip and the game of basketball!

FACTOR

Map labels:

GREENLAND
Ellesmere Island
izabeth Islands
Baffin Bay
Baffin Island
Davis Strait
NUNAVUT
Southampton Island
Hudson Strait
UNGAVA PENINSULA
Ungava Bay
Labrador Sea
Hudson Bay
NEWFOUNDLAND AND LABRADOR
Churchill
ANITOBA
Lake Winnipeg
ONTARIO
SHIELD
James Bay
QUÉBEC
LAURENTIAN MOUNTAINS
Anticosti Island
Gulf of St Lawrence
Newfoundland
ST PIERRE & MIQUELON (to France)
PRINCE EDWARD ISLAND
NEW BRUNSWICK
Lake Superior
Lake Michigan
Lake Huron
OTTAWA
St Lawrence
Bay of Fundy
NOVA SCOTIA
ATLANTIC OCEAN
Lake Ontario
Niagara Falls
Lake Erie
ICA

United States of America

The United States of America is one of the richest countries in the world. It is almost the size of Europe. There are huge mountain ranges, grasslands, forests and hot deserts. In Alaska, in the north, snow and ice cover the ground all year round. Many people live in the USA, especially on the east coast.

NORTH

WEST   EAST

SOUTH

CANADA

PACIFIC

WASHINGTON

MONTANA   Missouri

OREGON

IDAHO

Yellowstone National Park

1

WYOMING

UNITED

Great Salt Lake

NEVADA

CALIFORNIA

UTAH

COLORADO

Colorado

Grand Canyon

Monument Valley

2

ARIZONA

NEW MEXICO

OF

OCEAN

MEXICO

GREAT P

RUSS. FED.

BROOKS RANGE

Arctic Circle

Yukon

ALASKA

Mount McKinley (Denali) 6194m

CANADA

0   400 km

0   200 miles

Aleutian Islands

Gulf of Alaska

ROCKY MOUNTAINS

1 Old Faithful

More than half of all the hot water geysers in the world are in Yellowstone National Park. The most famous is 'Old Faithful'.

Kauai

HAWAII

Oahu

PACIFIC OCEAN

Maui

0   200 km   Hawaii

0   200 miles

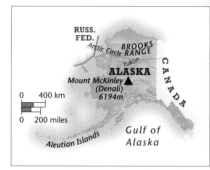

2 Rattlesnake

This snake has a rattle on its tail which makes a buzzing sound as a warning. The snake bites its prey and kills it with poisonous venom!

3 Rodeo

A rodeo is an exciting competition. Cowboys and cowgirls can show off their skill at riding horses and rounding up the cattle.

4 American bison

For thousands of years there were millions of bison living wild in northern America. Now there are only small herds of bison kept in some national parks.

0 200 400 kilometres

0 200 400 miles

CANADA

Lake Superior

MAINE

NORTH DAKOTA

MINNESOTA

MICHIGAN

Lake Huron

VERMONT

NEW HAMPSHIRE

SOUTH DAKOTA

WISCONSIN

Lake Michigan

Lake Ontario

NEW YORK

MASSACHUSETTS

STATES

Mississippi

IOWA

RHODE ISLAND

CONNECTICUT

Lake Erie

EBRASKA

PENNSYLVANIA

OHIO

INDIANA

NEW JERSEY

DELAWARE

ILLINOIS

Ohio

WEST VIRGINIA

MARYLAND

5 WASHINGTON DC

KANSAS

Missouri

KENTUCKY

APPALACHIAN MTS

VIRGINIA

MERICA

MISSOURI

TENNESSEE

NORTH CAROLINA

OKLAHOMA

ARKANSAS

Arkansas

Red River

3

MISSISSIPPI

SOUTH CAROLINA

ALABAMA

GEORGIA

EXAS

7

Mississippi

ATLANTIC OCEAN

LOUISIANA

FLORIDA

6

ande

Mississippi Delta

Gulf of Mexico

Lake Okeechobee

Florida Keys

5 The White House

The president of the United States of America lives and works at the famous White House in Washington DC. His office is called the Oval Office.

6 Space Shuttle

The world's most famous launch site for spacecraft such as the Space Shuttle is at the Kennedy Space Centre, in Florida. The Space Centre is very popular with tourists.

7 Paddle steamer

For over 150 years the steamboats of the Mississippi carried goods up and down the river. Now paddle steamers are used for tourists.

THE WOW!

The stars on the American flag represent the 50 states of the United States of America.

FACTOR

Central America and the Caribbean

Central America is where the huge continents of North America and South America join. There are lots of mountains and rainforests, and in the north are hot, dry deserts. Fishing and coffee-growing are important here, and tourism and sugar-farming are important on islands such as Jamaica.

2 Day of the Dead

Once a year in Mexico people have a celebration called the 'Day of the Dead'. They pray for and remember their relatives and friends who have died.

3 Mayan ruins

This Mayan temple is at Tikal in Guatemala. Over 1,000 years ago the city of Tikal was left by its people. It was discovered again in 1848, all overgrown and hidden by trees!

UNITED STATES OF AMERICA

Sonora
Desert

Baja California

Gulf of California

PACIFIC OCEAN

Yaqui

Conchos

SIERRA MADRE OCCIDENTAL

Río Grande

MEXICO

SIERRA MADRE ORIENTAL

Gulf of
Mexico

Tropic of Cancer

1 Ocelot

These wild cats live mainly in rainforest trees and they hunt at night. Ocelots can also swim well.

NORTH

WEST   EAST

SOUTH

1

★ MEXICO CITY

2

Balsas

SIERRA MADRE DEL SUR

Gulf of
Tehuantepec

YUCAT

3

GUATEMAL

GUATEMALA CITY ★

SAN SALVADOR

EL SALVADO

PACIFIC

5 Panama Canal

This long canal was built to link the Pacific and Atlantic oceans, so that ships do not have to travel all the way round South America.

4 Caribbean Sea

The Caribbean Sea is famous for its colourful corals and fishes. The warm water is home to all kinds of wildlife.

6 Classy Cuba

The capital city of Cuba is Havana. You can see lots of classic American cars in this city. Some of them are over 50 years old, but they still work!

THE WOW!

All the islands in the Caribbean were once owned by European countries, including Britain, France and Spain. The British Virgin Islands and Martinique still are!

FACTOR

ATLANTIC OCEAN

NASSAU ★
Andros Island
BAHAMAS

HAVANA ★ 6
CUBA

TURKS & CAICOS ISLANDS
(to UK)

BRITISH VIRGIN ISLANDS
(to UK)

VIRGIN ISLANDS
(to US)

Leeward Islands

GUANTANAMO BAY
(to US)

Greater

Isla Cozumel

PENINSULA

CAYMAN ISLANDS
(to UK)

HAITI
PORT-AU-PRINCE ★

DOMINICAN REPUBLIC

PUERTO RICO
(to US)

SAN JUAN ★

ANGUILLA
(to UK)

ANTIGUA & BARBUDA

Antilles

JAMAICA ★
KINGSTON

SANTO DOMINGO

ST KITTS & NEVIS

MONTSERRAT
(to UK)

GUADELOUPE
(to France)

DOMINICA

MARTINIQUE
(to France)

BELMOPAN
BELIZE 4

ST LUCIA

BARBADOS

HONDURAS
★ TEGUCIGALPA

Caribbean Sea

ARUBA
(to Netherlands)

CURACAO
(to Netherlands)

Lesser Antilles

Windward Islands

ST VINCENT & THE GRENADINES

GRENADA

Tobago

NICARAGUA
★ MANAGUA
Lake Nicaragua

VENEZUELA

TRINIDAD & TOBAGO
7

SAN JOSE ★

COSTA RICA

OCEAN

Panama Canal

Gulf of Darien

5
PANAMA CITY ★

PANAMA

COLOMBIA

0   250   500 kilometres

0   250   500 miles

7 Caribbean music

Trinidad and Tobago are famous for their loud steel band music. The first steel drums were made from old oil barrels.

North America country facts

There are 23 countries in North America and more than 200 different languages. Most of the people living here speak English, Spanish or French. There are more than 17 different kinds of currency in North America.

Canada
Capital City Ottawa
Population 33,759,742
Area 9,984,670 sq km
Main languages English, French
Money 1 Canadian dollar = 100 cents

Mexico
Capital City Mexico City (Distrito Federal)
Population 112,468,855
Area 1,964,375 sq km
Main languages Spanish
Money 1 peso = 100 centavos

Bahamas
Capital City Nassau
Population 310,426
Area 13,880 sq km
Main languages English
Money 1 Bahamian dollar = 100 cents

Belize
Capital City Belmopan
Population 314,522
Area 22,966 sq km
Main languages English, Spanish, Mayan, Garifuna (Carib), Creole
Money 1 Belizean dollar = 100 cents

United States of America
Capital City Washington DC
Population 310,232,863
Area 9,826,675 sq km
Main languages English
Money 1 US dollar = 100 cents

Cuba
Capital City Havana
Population 11,477,459
Area 110,860 sq km
Main languages Spanish
Money 1 Cuban peso = 100 centavos

Guatemala
Capital City Guatemala City
Population 13,550,440
Area 108,889 sq km
Main languages Spanish and more than 20 local languages
Money 1 quetzal = 100 centavos

Haiti
Capital City Port-au-Prince
Population 9,719,932
Area 27,750 sq km
Main languages Creole, French
Money 1 gourde = 100 centimes

El Salvador
Capital City San Salvador
Population 6,052,064
Area 21,041 sq km
Main languages Spanish
Money 1 US dollar = 100 cents

Emptiest country

The emptiest place in North America is Canada. It has lots of land and hardly any people. The most crowded place in North America is the Bahamas.

Honduras
Capital City Tegucigalpa
Population 7,989,415
Area 112,090 sq km
Main languages Spanish,
English and local languages
Money 1 lempira =
100 centavos

Dominican Republic
Capital City Santo Domingo
Population 9,823,821
Area 48,670 sq km
Main languages Spanish
Money 1 Dominican peso =
100 centavos

Nicaragua
Capital City Managua
Population 5,995,928
Area 130,370 sq km
Main languages Spanish,
English and local languages
Money 1 gold cordoba =
100 centavos

Jamaica
Capital City Kingston
Population 2,847,232

Area 10,991 sq km
Main languages English,
English patois
Money 1 Jamaican dollar =
100 cents

St Kitts and Nevis
Capital City Basseterre
Population 49,898
Area 261 sq km (St Kitts 168 sq km; Nevis 93 sq km)
Main languages English
Money 1 East Caribbean dollar = 100 cents

Antigua and Barbuda
Capital City Saint John's
Population 86,754
Area 442.6 sq km (Antigua 280 sq km; Barbuda 161 sq km)
Main languages English
Money 1 East Caribbean dollar = 100 cents

Costa Rica
Capital City San Jose
Population 4,516,220
Area 51,100 sq km
Main languages Spanish,
English
Money 1 Costa Rican colon =
100 centimos

The colourful Caribbean

The busy markets of the Caribbean are full of colourful fruit and vegetables. Jamaica, Barbados and the other islands are popular places to visit.

Panama
Capital City Panama City
Population 3,410,676
Area 75,420 sq km
Main languages Spanish,
English
Money 1 balboa = 100 cents

Dominica
Capital City Roseau
Population 72,813
Area 751 sq km
Main languages English,
French patois
Money 1 East Caribbean dollar = 100 cents

St Lucia
Capital City Castries
Population 160,922
Area 616 sq km
Main languages English,
French patois
Money 1 East Caribbean dollar = 100 cents

St Vincent and the Grenadines
Capital City Kingstown
Population 104,217

Area 389 sq km (St Vincent 344 sq km)
Main languages English
Money 1 East Caribbean dollar = 100 cents

Barbados
Capital City Bridgetown
Population 285,653
Area 430 sq km
Main languages English, Bajan
Money 1 Barbadian dollar =
100 cents

Grenada
Capital City Saint George's
Population 107,818
Area 344 sq km
Main languages English,
French patois
Money 1 East Caribbean dollar = 100 cents

Trinidad and Tobago
Capital City Port-of-Spain
Population 1,228,691
Area 5,128 sq km
Main languages English
Money 1 Trinidad and Tobago dollar = 100 cents

US DOLLARS

⭐ The United States dollar is the official currency of the United States of America. It is the world's most important currency, and it is used everywhere for trading gold and oil. Several other countries also use US dollars as their official currency.

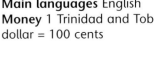

South America

This is the fourth-largest continent in the world. South America has 12 countries. The biggest country is Brazil and the smallest is Suriname. Brazil takes up almost half of all the land in South America. It has more people than any of the other countries. Lots of Europeans moved here about 500 years ago and most people speak Spanish or Portuguese.

ECUADOR

Biggest forest

Earth's largest rainforest is in South America. More than half of the rainforest is in Brazil. It also covers land that belongs to eight other countries. Brazil has the huge River Amazon too. This is the largest river on Earth!

Smallest country

Suriname is the smallest country in South America. It is close to the Equator so it has a very hot tropical climate. Most of the people speak several languages, including Dutch.

Longest country

Chile is the world's longest country. In the north are the high Andes mountains, which are all the way down South America. This is the biggest range of mountains on Earth.

COLOMBIA

VENEZUELA

GUYANA
SURINAME
FRENCH GUIANA
(to France)

P E R U

B R A Z I L

BOLIVIA

PACIFIC
OCEAN

PARAGUAY

C H I L E

A R G E N T I N A

ATLANTIC
OCEAN

URUGUAY

NORTH

WEST   EAST

SOUTH

FALKLAND
ISLANDS
(to UK)

THE WOW!

Potatoes first came from the Andes, in South America. The Incas were the first people to farm them. They dried the potatoes and then turned them into flour.

FACTOR

Biggest city

The huge, modern Brazilian city of Sao Paulo is the largest city in South America. Sao Paulo has a population of more than 11 million people.

ABOUT SOUTH AMERICA

NUMBER OF COUNTRIES	12
SIZE	World's 4th-largest continent
TOTAL AREA	17,840,000 sq kilometres
POPULATION	385,742,554 million people
BIGGEST COUNTRY	Brazil – 8,514,877 square kilometres
SMALLEST COUNTRY	Suriname – total area 163,820 square kilometres
BIGGEST CITY	Sao Paulo, Brazil

South America

Most of South America is warm, but in the far south and high in the Andes mountains it is colder. The great Amazon river flows through the world's biggest tropical rainforest. In the south millions of cattle graze on grasslands. Most of the people in South America live in cities near the coast.

1 Angel Falls

The world's highest waterfall is Angels Falls in Venezuela. It is two-and-a-half times as high as the Empire State Building in New York, USA!

3 Machu Picchu

High up in the Andes mountains are the ruins of the ancient Inca city of Machu Picchu. The city was built in about 1450 but it was abondoned 100 years later. Now it is a world-famous monument.

2 Scarlet macaws

These colourful birds live in the rainforest. They are popular as pets, but people are not allowed to catch them now without a special licence.

4 Jaguar

The jaguar is the third-largest cat in the world, after lions and tigers. Jaguars live mostly in rainforests and are in danger of extinction.

5 Galapagos tortoise

The world's biggest tortoises live on the Galapagos Islands. They can weigh as much as five men!

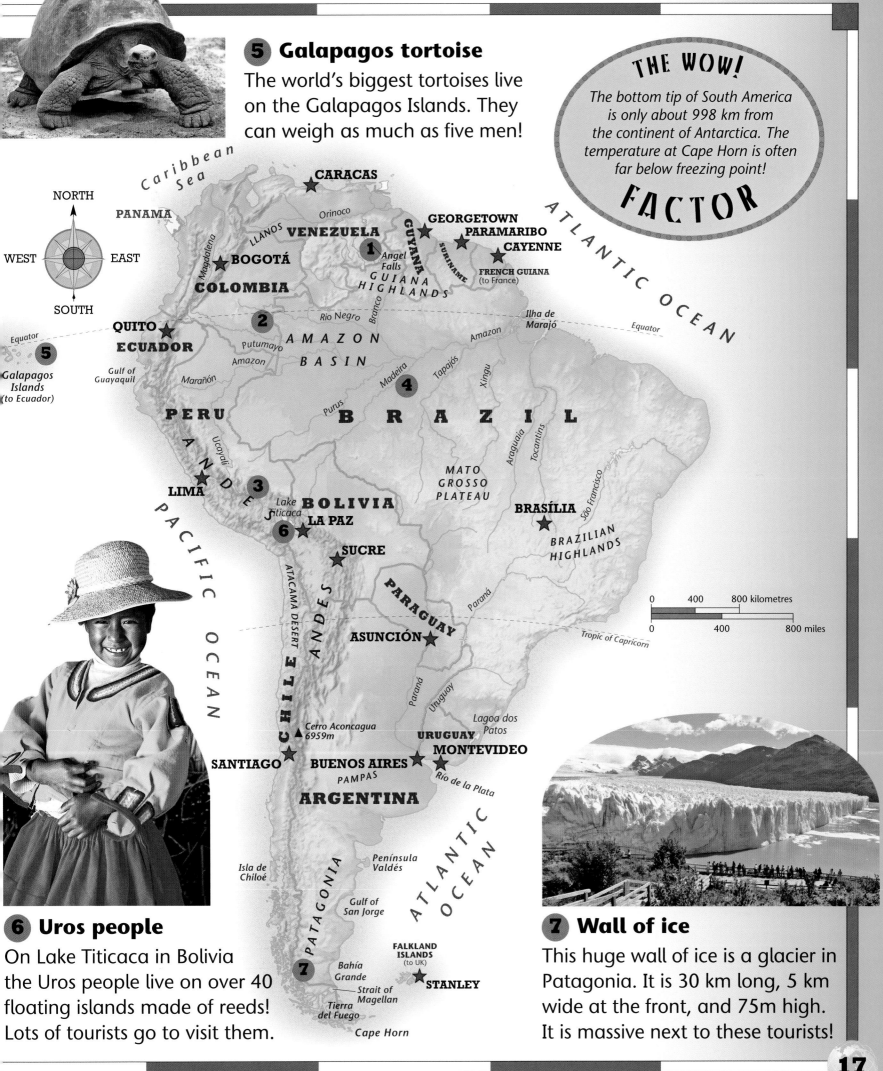

NORTH
WEST EAST
SOUTH

Caribbean Sea

PANAMA

CARACAS

Orinoco

LLANOS

VENEZUELA

Magdalena

BOGOTÁ

COLOMBIA

GUYANA

GEORGETOWN
PARAMARIBO
CAYENNE

Angel Falls

GUIANA HIGHLANDS

SURINAME

FRENCH GUIANA (to France)

ATLANTIC OCEAN

Equator

QUITO
ECUADOR

Putumayo

Amazon

Rio Negro

Branco

AMAZON BASIN

Amazon

Ilha de Marajó

Equator

Galapagos Islands (to Ecuador)

Gulf of Guayaquil

Marañón

Madeira

Purus

Tapajós

Xingu

PERU

B R A Z I L

Ucayali

Lake Titicaca

BOLIVIA

LA PAZ

SUCRE

MATO GROSSO PLATEAU

Araguaia

Tocantins

BRASÍLIA

São Francisco

BRAZILIAN HIGHLANDS

LIMA

A N D E S

PACIFIC OCEAN

ATACAMA DESERT

PARAGUAY

Paraná

ASUNCIÓN

Tropic of Capricorn

Cerro Aconcagua 6959m

CHILE

Paraná

Uruguay

URUGUAY

MONTEVIDEO

Lagoa dos Patos

SANTIAGO

BUENOS AIRES

PAMPAS

Río de la Plata

ARGENTINA

Isla de Chiloé

Península Valdés

PATAGONIA

Gulf of San Jorge

ATLANTIC OCEAN

FALKLAND ISLANDS (to UK)

Bahía Grande

STANLEY

Strait of Magellan

Tierra del Fuego

Cape Horn

0   400   800 kilometres
0   400   800 miles

6 Uros people

On Lake Titicaca in Bolivia the Uros people live on over 40 floating islands made of reeds! Lots of tourists go to visit them.

7 Wall of ice

This huge wall of ice is a glacier in Patagonia. It is 30 km long, 5 km wide at the front, and 75m high. It is massive next to these tourists!

South America country facts

There are 12 countries in South America and about 350 languages are spoken. The most widely spoken languages are Portuguese and Spanish. There are 13 currencies in South America, including the euro, which is used in French Guiana.

Colombia
Capital City Bogota
Population 44,205,293
Area 1,138,910 sq km
Main languages Spanish
Money 1 Colombian peso = 100 centavos

Venezuela
Capital City Caracas
Population 27,223,228
Area 912,050 sq km
Main languages Spanish and local languages
Money 1 bolivar = 100 centimos

Guyana
Capital City Georgetown
Population 748,486
Area 214,969 sq km
Main languages English, Creole, Hindi, Urdu and local languages
Money 1 Guyanese dollar = 100 cents

Suriname
Capital City Paramaribo
Population 486,618
Area 163,820 sq km
Main languages Dutch, English, Sranang Tongo, Hindi, Javanese
Money 1 Suriname dollar = 100 cents

Ecuador
Capital City Quito
Population 14,790,608
Area 283,561 sq km
Main languages Spanish, local languages
Money 1 US dollar = 100 cents

Peru
Capital City Lima
Population 29,907,003
Area 1,285,216 sq km
Main languages Spanish, Quechua, Aymara
Money 1 nuevo sol = 100 centimos

Brazil
Capital City Brasilia
Population 201,103,330
Area 8,514,877 sq km
Main languages Portuguese
Money 1 real = 100 centavos

Bolivia
Capital City La Paz and Sucre
Population 9,947,418
Area 1,098,581 sq km
Main languages Spanish, Quechua, Aymara, Guarani
Money 1 boliviano = 100 centavos

Busy Bolivia

The population of Bolivia includes Amerindians, Asians, Mestizos, Europeans and Africans. Most of the people speak Spanish, but there are also over 35 local languages.

A country called Colombia

Columbia is named after the explorer Christopher Columbus, although he never actually visited here. It was his companion, Alonso de Ojeda, who was the first European to land here in 1499.

Wealthy capital

Santiago is the capital of Chile. This modern city has become a rich, important trading place in the last 50 years. It has smart offices and shopping malls, and attractive areas where people can live.

Colourful houses

The capital of Argentina is Buenos Aires. Some of the older houses are painted in jolly colours. The city has grown much larger in the last 100 years. Over 15 million people live here now!

Paraguay
Capital City Asuncion
Population 6,375,830
Area 406,752 sq km
Main languages Spanish, Guarani
Money 1 guarani = 100 centimos

Uruguay
Capital City Montevideo
Population 3,510,386
Area 176,215 sq km
Main languages Spanish, Portunol, Brazilero
Money 1 Uruguayan peso = 100 centesimos

Chile
Capital City Santiago
Population 16,746,491
Area 756,102 sq km
Main languages Spanish
Money 1 Chilean peso = 100 centavos

Argentina
Capital City Buenos Aires
Population 41,343,201
Area 2,780,400 sq km
Main languages Spanish
Money 1 peso = 100 centavos

RIO CARNIVAL

☆ Many Catholic countries around the world have a carnival every year at the beginning of Lent. This is 40 days before Easter. The biggest and most famous of these carnivals is in Brazil. The celebrations carry on through the day and night in every town and city. The country stops completely for almost a week for the party!

Dancers having fun at the Rio Carnival in Brazil

Africa

This is the second-biggest continent in the world. Africa has 55 countries and thousands of different languages. It also has the biggest desert in the world, called the Sahara. Hardly any people live in the desert because it is too hot. Most of the people live near the coast or along the banks of rivers.

Biggest city

Africa's biggest city is Cairo, in Egypt. Almost 17 million people live here. Its nickname is 'city of 1,000 minarets'. You can see the tall minarets in this picture.

CAPE VERDE

GAMBIA

GUINEA-BISSAU

Biggest country

Sudan used to be the biggest single country in Africa, but now it has split into two countries. Southern Sudan will have its own capital city, called Juba. So now Algeria is Africa's biggest country!

ABOUT AFRICA

NUMBER OF COUNTRIES	55
SIZE	World's 2nd-largest continent
TOTAL AREA	30,221,532 sq kilometres
POPULATION	1.1 billion people
BIGGEST COUNTRY	Algeria – 2,381,741 square kilometres
SMALLEST COUNTRY	Seychelles – total area 451 square kilometres
BIGGEST CITY	Cairo, Egypt

High country

The highest country in the world is Lesotho, in South Africa. It is also one of the world's poorest countries. Most of the people here are farmers.

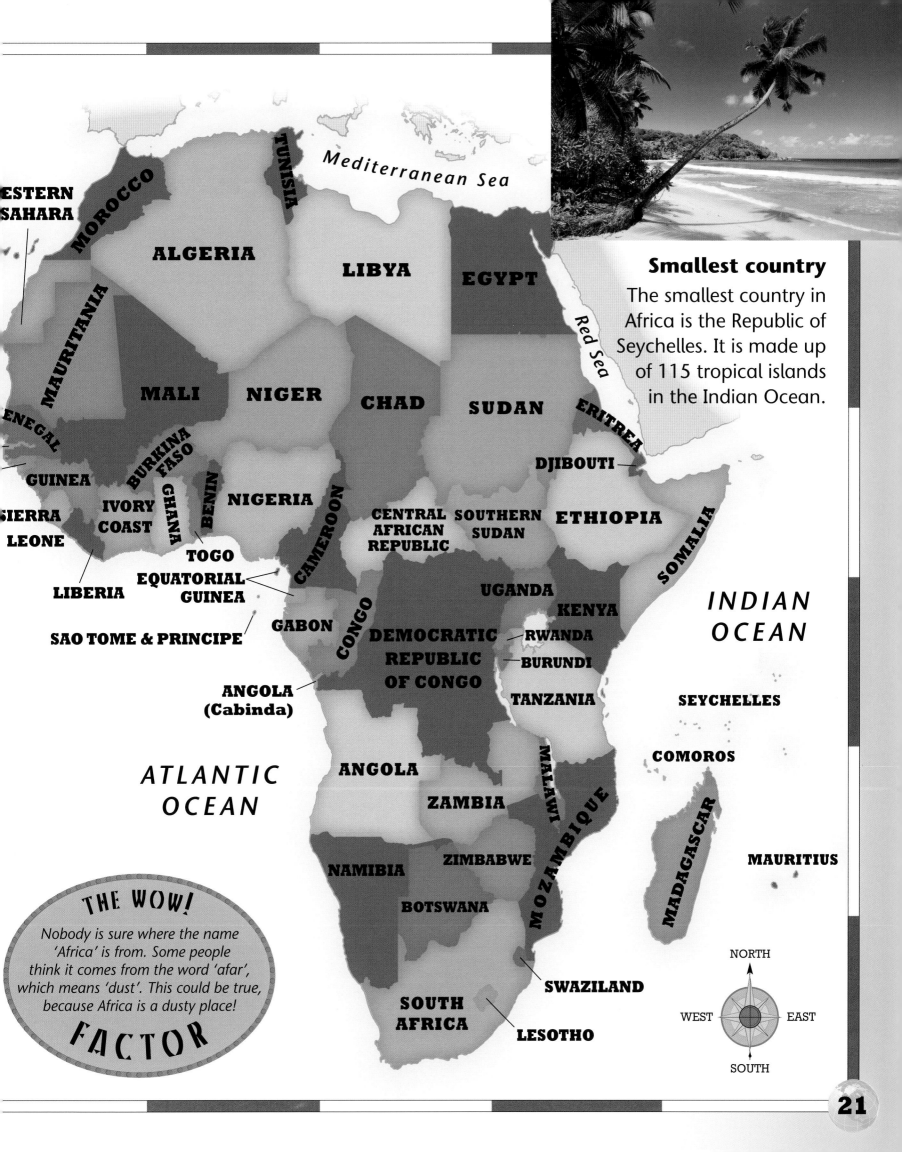

WESTERN SAHARA

MOROCCO

TUNISIA

Mediterranean Sea

ALGERIA

LIBYA

EGYPT

MAURITANIA

MALI

NIGER

CHAD

SUDAN

Red Sea

ERITREA

SENEGAL

BURKINA FASO

DJIBOUTI

GUINEA

IVORY COAST

GHANA

BENIN

NIGERIA

CENTRAL AFRICAN REPUBLIC

SOUTHERN SUDAN

ETHIOPIA

SIERRA LEONE

TOGO

CAMEROON

SOMALIA

LIBERIA

EQUATORIAL GUINEA

UGANDA

SAO TOME & PRINCIPE

GABON

CONGO

DEMOCRATIC REPUBLIC OF CONGO

RWANDA

KENYA

BURUNDI

INDIAN OCEAN

ANGOLA (Cabinda)

TANZANIA

SEYCHELLES

ATLANTIC OCEAN

ANGOLA

ZAMBIA

MALAWI

MOZAMBIQUE

COMOROS

MADAGASCAR

MAURITIUS

NAMIBIA

ZIMBABWE

BOTSWANA

SWAZILAND

SOUTH AFRICA

LESOTHO

Smallest country

The smallest country in Africa is the Republic of Seychelles. It is made up of 115 tropical islands in the Indian Ocean.

THE WOW!

Nobody is sure where the name 'Africa' is from. Some people think it comes from the word 'afar', which means 'dust'. This could be true, because Africa is a dusty place!

FACTOR

NORTH

WEST — EAST

SOUTH

Northern Africa

Almost all of Northern Africa is covered by the huge Sahara desert. Life in the desert is difficult. Most people in Northern Africa live along the River Nile or close to the sea. This area is very hot, so it is perfect for growing grapes, olives, dates and cocoa. Lots of tourists visit Northern Africa, and tourism is important because it brings money to many poor areas.

1 Colourful carpets

In many parts of Northern Africa people make colourful rugs and carpets. Lots of these are sold to tourists, especially in Morocco and Tunisia.

NORTH
WEST   EAST
SOUTH

Mediter...

ALGIERS ★   TUNIS ★
RABAT ★
MOROCCO   ATLAS MOUNTAINS   TUNISIA
LAAYOUNE ★   ALGERIA
WESTERN SAHARA
Tropic of Cancer   4   AHAGGAR
S A H A R A
MAURITANIA
NOUAKCHOTT ★   MALI   NIGER
CAPE VERDE
PRAIA ★   SENEGAL   *Senegal*   S A H E L
DAKAR ★   2   NIAMEY ★
GAMBIA   BAMAKO ★   *Niger*
BANJUL   OUAGADOUGOU ★
BISSAU   BURKINA FASO   NIGERI
GUINEA-BISSAU   GUINEA   NIGERI
CONAKRY ★   3   IVORY   ABUJA ★
FREETOWN ★   COAST   PORTO-NOVO
SIERRA LEONE   YAMOUSSOUKRO   GHANA TOGO BENIN
MONROVIA ★   LOME   YAOUNDE
LIBERIA   ACCRA
Gulf of Guinea
EQUATORIAL GUINEA

0   400   800 kilometres
0   400   800 miles

2 Dogon dancer

This man belongs to the Dogon tribe, from Mali. He is wearing an antelope mask. His tribe keep most of their dances and ceremonies a secret, but visitors are allowed to watch them do their antelope dance.

3 Little hippo

Small pygmy hippopotamuses live in the forests of Sierra Leone and the Ivory Coast. They are only 75 cm high and weigh 250 kg. Ordinary hippos are over 1.5 m high and weigh over 3,000 kg!

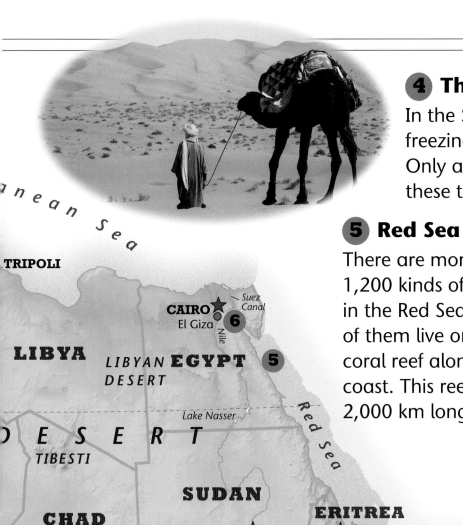

4 The Sahara desert

In the Sahara the temperature is often below freezing at night and over 40°C during the day. Only a few people and animals can put up with these temperatures and the harsh conditions.

5 Red Sea

There are more than 1,200 kinds of fishes in the Red Sea. Most of them live on the coral reef along the coast. This reef is 2,000 km long!

THE WOW!

The biggest hot desert in the world is the Sahara. It has an area of over nine million square kilometres. That is about the same size as the whole of Europe!

FACTOR

TRIPOLI

CAIRO ★ Suez Canal
El Giza ○ 6

LIBYA   LIBYAN EGYPT   5
         DESERT

Lake Nasser

DESERT   Red Sea

TIBESTI

SUDAN

CHAD   KHARTOUM ★   ERITREA
                      ★ ASMARA

Lake Chad   Darfur   Blue Nile

★NDJAMENA   DJIBOUTI
             ★ DJIBOUTI

ETHIOPIAN   HORN OF
             AFRICA

SUDD   7 ★ADDIS ABABA

CENTRAL   SOUTHERN   HIGHLANDS
AFRICAN   SUDAN   ETHIOPIA
REPUBLIC   JUBA ★

BANGUI ★   SOMALIA

DEMOCRATIC REPUBLIC   Lake Turkana
OF CONGO   UGANDA   KENYA

CONGO   ★ MOGADISHU

                INDIAN OCEAN

6 Egyptian pyramids

These pyramids are at El Giza, on the edge of the Sahara. They were built 4,000 years ago, and are tombs. The biggest is the Great Pyramid. Nobody knows exactly how they were made.

7 Ethiopian wolf

This wolf lives in the highlands of Ethiopia. There are less than 600 of these endangered wolves left in the wild.

Southern Africa

The southern part of Africa includes the hot desert of Namibia, a tropical rainforest around the Congo and grasslands and forests. Most of the well-known African animals, such as elephants, lions, rhinoceroses and gorillas, live here. There are lots more people in Southern Africa than Northern Africa, with hundreds of tribes speaking many languages.

1 Mega sand dunes

One of the hottest and driest places on Earth is the Namib Desert. This enormous desert is more than 50 million years old. In the middle of the desert are the tallest sand dunes in the world. They are over 300 m high!

2 Groups of gorillas

Gorillas are the largest kind of ape. They live in groups in the forests of Rwanda and the Congo. These mammals can live for more than 35 years.

3 Flowers in the desert

Every year after the winter rain, millions of colourful flowers on the dry west coast of South Africa bloom for a few weeks. Local people call this the 'daisy season'.

MALABO ⭐
EQUATORIAL GUINEA
CAMEROON
CENTRAL AFRIC
Ubang
Cong
2
CON
BAS
SAO TOME ⭐
SAO TOME & PRINCIPE
⭐ LIBREVILLE
GABON
CONGO
Congo
DEM
RE
BRAZZAVILLE
⭐ KINSHASA
O
ANGOLA
LUANDA ⭐
ATLANTIC OCEAN
ANGOLA
BIÉ PLATEAU
Zam
Okavango
NAMIBIA
WINDHOEK
⭐ KALAHA
NAMIB DESERT
1 DESER
Orange River
3
SOUT
CAPE TOWN ⭐
Cape of Good Hope

4 Elephants in Africa

There are over 2,000 elephants in the Serengeti National Park. This is one of the biggest groups of protected elephants in Africa.

5 Maasai mud huts

The Maasai people of Kenya and Tanzania live in traditional round houses made of mud, grass, wood and cow dung. Maasai houses are usually built by the women.

PUBLIC
SUDAN
ETHIOPIA
Lake Turkana
SOMALIA
UGANDA
KAMPALA
KENYA
Equator
5
RATIC
KIGALI
RWANDA
Lake Victoria
GREAT RIFT VALLEY
NAIROBI
BLIC
BUJUMBURA
BURUNDI
▲ Kilimanjaro 5895m
ONGO
Lake Tanganyika
GREAT RIFT VALLEY
DODOMA
4
SEYCHELLES
TANZANIA
MALAWI
Lake Nyasa
COMOROS
MORONI
LILONGWE
MAYOTTE (to France)
ZAMBIA
LUSAKA
Zambezi
Victoria Falls
HARARE
6
ZIMBABWE
7
MADAGASCAR
ANTANANARIVO
MOZAMBIQUE
Mozambique Channel
MAURITIUS
PORT LOUIS
RÉUNION (to France)
BOTSWANA
GABORONE
Limpopo
Tropic of Capricorn
TSHWANE (PRETORIA)
MAPUTO
SWAZILAND
MBABANE
BLOEMFONTEIN
MASERU
LESOTHO
FRICA
INDIAN OCEAN

NORTH
WEST — EAST
SOUTH

0   400   800 kilometres
0   400   800 miles

THE WOW! FACTOR

There are more than 2,000 different languages in Africa. Many African people can speak more than one language.

6 Victoria Falls

This famous waterfall is 108 m high and 1,700 m wide. Many people say that this is one of the seven natural wonders of the world.

7 Colourful chameleon

The pretty 'Panther' chameleons from Madagascar are different colours depending on where they live. They can be blue, red, green or orange!

Africa country facts

There are 55 countries in Africa and over 2,000 languages. Many of these languages belong to different tribes, so only a few people know how to speak them well. Africa has 42 official currencies. Many countries use US dollars and euros for trading abroad.

Morocco
Capital City Rabat
Population 31,627,428
Area 446,550 sq km
Main languages Arabic, Berber, French, Spanish
Money 1 dirham = 100 centimes

Algeria
Capital City Algiers
Population 34,586,184
Area 281,741 sq km
Main languages Arabic, French, Berber
Money 1 dinar = 100 centimes

Tunisia
Capital City Tunis
Population 10,589,025
Area 163,610 sq km
Main languages Arabic, French
Money 1 Tunisian dinar = 1,000 millimes

Libya
Capital City Tripoli (Tarabulus)
Population 6,461,454
Area 1,759,540 sq km
Main languages Arabic
Money 1 Libyan dinar = 1,000 dirhams

Egypt
Capital City Cairo
Population 80,471,869
Area 1,001,450 sq km
Main languages Arabic
Money 1 Egyptian pound = 100 piastres

Mauritania
Capital City Nouakchott
Population 3,205,060
Area 1,030,700 sq km
Main languages Arabic, French
Money 1 ouguiya = 5 khoums

Mali
Capital City Bamako
Population 13,796,354
Area 1,240,192 sq km
Main languages French, Bambara, Berber, Arabic
Money 1 CFA (Communaute Financiere Africaine) franc = 100 centimes

Niger
Capital City Niamey
Population 15,878,271
Area 1,267,000 sq km
Main languages French, Arabic, Hausa, Songhai
Money 1 CFA (Communaute Financiere Africaine) franc = 100 centimes

Chad
Capital City N'Djamena
Population 10,543,464
Area 1,284,000 sq km
Main languages French, Arabic
Money 1 CFA (Communaute Financiere Africaine) franc = 100 centimes

Sudan
Capital City Khartoum
Population 35,679,598 (estimated)
Area 1,916,068 sq km (estimated)
Main languages Arabic, English
Money 1 Sudanese pound = 100 qirsh

Southern Sudan
Capital City Juba
Population 8,260,000 (estimated)
Area 589,745 sq km (estimated)
Main languages English, Arabic (Juba Arabic)

Majestic mud

The Great Mosque at Djenne in Mali is the largest mud building in the world. It was built in 1907, and is made out of mud bricks covered with mud plaster. This type of mud building is called an 'adobe' building. People still build mud houses in many countries.

Money 1 Sudanese pound = 100 qirsh

Western Sahara
Capital City Laayoune
Population 491,519
Area 266,000 sq km
Main languages Hassaniya Arabic, Moroccan Arabic
Money Moroccan dirham = 100 Santim

Burkina Faso
Capital City Ouagadougou
Population 16,241,811
Area 274,200 sq km
Main languages French and local languages
Money 1 CFA (Communaute Financiere Africaine) franc = 100 centimes

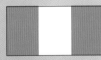

Nigeria
Capital City Abuja
Population 152,217,341
Area 923,768 sq km
Main languages English, Yoruba, Ibo, Hausa
Money 1 Nigerian naira = 100 kobo

Cameroon
Capital City Yaounde
Population 19,294,149
Area 475,440 sq km
Main languages French, English, languages of Bantu, Semi-Bantu and Sudanic groups
Money 1 CFA (Communaute Financiere Africaine) franc = 100 centimes

Central African Republic
Capital City Bangui

Lively Morocco

This is the old city of Marrakesh, in Morocco. It is a lively, colourful place and lots of tourists come here. Morocco is very close to Europe and it is a cheap place to travel to. People enjoy the interesting crafts, food and the warm climate.

Population 4,844,927
Area 622,984 sq km
Main languages French, Sangho (lingua franca)
Money 1 CFA (Communaute Financiere Africaine) franc = 100 centimes

Ethiopia
Capital City Addis Ababa
Population 88,013,491
Area 1,104,300 sq km
Main languages Amharic, Oromo, Tigrinya, Somali
Money 1 birr = 100 cents

Eritrea
Capital City Asmara (Asmera)
Population 5,792,984
Area 117,600 sq km
Main languages Tigrinya, Tigre, Arabic, English
Money 1 nakfa = 100 cents

Djibouti
Capital City Djibouti
Population 740,528
Area 23,200 sq km
Main languages French, Arabic, Somali, Afar
Money 1 Djiboutian franc = 100 centimes

Cape Verde
Capital City Praia
Population 508,659
Area 4,033 sq km
Main languages Portuguese, Crioulo (a mixture of archaic Portuguese and African words)
Money 1 Cape Verdean escudo = 100 centavos

Senegal
Capital City Dakar
Population 12,323,252
Area 196,722 sq km
Main languages French, Wolof
Money 1 CFA (Communaute Financiere Africaine) franc = 100 centimes

Ghana
Capital City Accra
Population 24,339,838
Area 238,533 sq km
Main languages English, African languages including Akan, Ewe
Money 1 cedi = 100 pesewa

Togo
Capital City Lome
Population 6,587,239
Area 56,785 sq km
Main languages French and local languages
Money 1 CFA (Communaute Financiere Africaine) franc = 100 centimes

Benin
Capital City Porto-Novo
Population 9,056,010
Area 112,622 sq km
Main languages French, Fon, Ge, Bariba, Yoruba, Dendi
Money 1 CFA (Communaute Financiere Africaine) franc = 100 centimes

Uganda
Capital City Kampala
Population 33,398,682
Area 241,038 sq km
Main languages English, Swahili, Luganda, various Bantu and Nilotic languages
Money 1 Ugandan shilling = 100 cents

Cattle farming

In Kenya and Tanzania cattle farming is very important. In these countries farmers such as the Maasai herd their cattle across the deserts and scrubland.

Kenya
Capital City Nairobi
Population 40,046,566
Area 580,367 sq km
Main languages Swahili, English
Money 1 Kenya shilling = 100 cents

Somalia
Capital City Mogadishu
Population 10,112,453
Area 637,657 sq km
Main languages Somali, Arabic, Italian, English
Money 1 Somali shilling = 100 cents

Gambia
Capital City Banjul
Population 1,824,158
Area 11,295 sq km
Main languages English, Mandinka, Wolof, Fula
Money 1 dalasi = 100 butut

Guinea-Bissau
Capital City Bissau
Population 1,565,126
Area 36,125 sq km
Main languages Portuguese, Crioulo, African languages
Money 1 CFA (Communaute Financiere Africaine) = 100 centimes

Guinea
Capital City Conakry
Population 10,324,025
Area 245,857 sq km
Main languages French, Susu, Fulani, Mandingo
Money 1 Guinean franc = 100 centimes

Rwanda
Capital City Kigali
Population 11,055,976
Area 26,338 sq km
Main languages Kinyarwanda, French, English, Swahili
Money 1 Rwandan franc = 100 centimes

Tanzania
Capital City Dodoma
Population 41,892,895
Area 947,300 sq km
Main languages English, Swahili
Money 1 Tanzanian shilling = 100 cents

Seychelles
Capital City Victoria
Population 88,340
Area 455 sq km
Main languages English, French, Creole
Money 1 Seychelles rupee = 100 cents

Sierra Leone
Capital City Freetown
Population 5,245,695
Area 71,740 sq km
Main languages English, Krio (Creole language derived from English) and a range of African languages
Money 1 leone = 100 cents

Liberia
Capital City Monrovia
Population 3,685,076
Area 111,369 sq km
Main languages English and about 29 local African languages
Money 1 Liberian dollar = 100 cents

Ivory Coast
Capital City Yamoussoukro
Population 20,617,068
Area 322,460 sq km
Main languages French and local languages
Money 1 CFA (Communaute Financiere Africaine) franc = 100 centimes

Democratic Republic of the Congo
Capital City Kinshasa
Population 70,916,439
Area 2,344,858 sq km
Main languages French, Lingala, Kiswahili, Kikongo, Tshiluba
Money 1 Congolese franc = 100 centimes

Burundi
Capital City Bujumbura
Population 9,863,117
Area 27,830 sq km
Main languages Kirundi, French, Swahili
Money 1 Burundi franc = 100 centimes

Equatorial Guinea
Capital City Malabo
Population 650,702
Area 28,051 sq km
Main languages Spanish, French
Money 1 CFA (Communaute Financiere Africaine) franc = 100 centimes

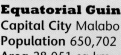

Gabon
Capital City Libreville
Population 1,545,255
Area 267,667 sq km
Main languages French, Bantu-group languages
Money 1 CFA (Communaute Financiere Africaine) franc = 100 centimes

Congo (Republic of the)
Capital City Brazzaville
Population 4,125,916
Area 342,000 sq km
Main languages French and local African languages
Money 1 CFA (Communaute Financiere Africaine) franc = 100 centimes

Malawi
Capital City Lilongwe
Population 15,447,500
Area 118,484 sq km
Main languages English, Chichewa
Money 1 Malawi kwacha = 100 tambala

Mozambique
Capital City Maputo
Population 22,061,451
Area 799,380 sq km
Main languages Portuguese, Makua-Lomwe, Swahili and other local languages
Money 1 metical = 100 centavos

Sao Tome and Principe
Capital City Sao Tome
Population 175,808
Area 964 sq km
Main languages Portuguese
Money 1 dobra = 100 centimos

Angola
Capital City Luanda
Population 13,068,161
Area 1,246,700 sq km
Main languages Portuguese, Umbundu, Kimbundu, Kikongo
Money 1 kwanza = 100 lwei

Zambia
Capital City Lusaka
Population 13,460,305
Area 752,618 sq km
Main languages English, Bemba, Lozi, Nyanja, Tonga
Money 1 kwacha = 100 ngwee

Zimbabwe
Capital City Harare
Population 11,651,858
Area 390,757 sq km
Main languages English, Shona, Sindebele
Money 1 Zimbabwe dollar = 100 cents

Madagascar
Capital City Antananarivo
Population 21,281,844
Area 587,041 sq km
Main languages Malagasy, French
Money 1 ariary = 5 iraimbilanja

Comoros
Capital City Moroni
Population 773,407
Area 2,235 sq km
Main languages Arabic, French, Comoran (a blend of Swahili and Arabic)
Money 1 Comoran franc = 100 centimes

Namibia
Capital City Windhoek
Population 2,128,471
Area 824,292 sq km
Main languages English, Afrikaans, German, Oshivambo, Herero, Nama
Money 1 Namibian dollar = 100 cents

Botswana
Capital City Gaborone
Population 2,029,307
Area 581,730 sq km
Main languages English, Setswana
Money 1 pula = 100 thebe

South Africa
Capital City Pretoria
Population 49,109,107
Area 1,219,090 sq km
Main languages 11 official languages including English, Afrikaans, Sesotho, Setswana, Xhosa and Zulu
Money 1 rand = 100 cents

Lesotho
Capital City Maseru
Population 1,919,522
Area 30,355 sq km
Main languages Sesotho, English
Money 1 loti = 100 lisente

Swaziland
Capital City Mbabane
Population 1,354,051
Area 17,364 sq km
Main languages Swazi, English
Money 1 lilangeni = 100 cents

Mauritius
Capital City Port Louis
Population 1,294,104
Area 2,040 sq km
Main languages English, Creole, French, Indian languages
Money 1 Mauritian rupee = 100 cents

SOUTH AFRICAN GOLD

☆ More than 30% of all the gold in the world has come from the gold mines in South Africa. The most common gold coin is the South African Kruggerand. This coin was first used in 1967 as a way to help ordinary people to own gold more easily. The Kruggerand contains a mixture of gold and copper. The copper helps to stop the coins from getting scratched and dented.

The Kruggerand coin is named after Paul Kruger, who was president of the old South African Republic. His picture is on one side of the coin. On the other side is a springbok, which is a symbol of South Africa.

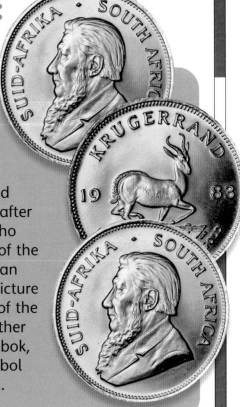

Europe

Europe is the fifth-largest continent in the world. It contains 46 countries. More than 730 million people live in Europe, speaking many different languages. The biggest country in the world is Russia. Part of Russia is in Europe and the rest of Russia is in Asia. Europe also contains the smallest country in the world, which is the Vatican City!

Biggest country

The biggest country in Europe is Russia. Large areas are covered in forest. People use planes to deliver things to each other!

Smallest country

The Vatican City is the tiniest country in Europe. It is inside Italy, and it contains St Peter's Basilica and the Apostolic Palace, where the Pope lives.

ICELAND

Norwegian Sea

NORWAY
SWEDEN
FINLAND

North Sea

ESTONIA
LATVIA
LITHUANIA

UNITED KINGDOM

DENMARK

RUSSIA

IRELAND

NETHERLANDS

BELARUS

POLAND

GERMANY

BELGIUM

CZECH REPUBLIC

UKRAINE

LUXEMBOURG
LIECHTENSTEIN

SLOVAKIA

FRANCE SWITZ.

AUSTRIA

HUNGARY

MOLDOVA

SLOVENIA

ROMANIA

SAN MARINO

CROATIA

SERBIA

MONACO

B&H

VATICAN CITY

MONTENEGRO

BULGARIA

Bla[c]

KOSOVO

MACEDONIA

ANDORRA

PORTUGAL   SPAIN

ITALY

ALBANIA

Mediterranean Sea

GREECE

MALTA

NORTH

WEST ● EAST

SOUTH

Barents Sea

RUSSIA

THE WOW!

Europe is named after Princess Europa, from Greek mythology. She was so beautiful that Zeus, the king of the gods, fell in love with her.

FACTOR

ea

Abbreviations:
B&H **Bosnia and Herzegovina**
SWITZ. **Switzerland**

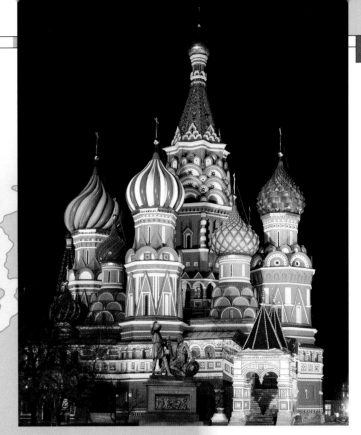

Biggest city

Moscow is Europe's biggest city. It is also the seventh-largest city in the world and is a mega city. Mega cities have a population with over 10 million people.

ABOUT EUROPE

NUMBER OF COUNTRIES	46
SIZE	World's 5th-largest continent
TOTAL AREA	10,531,000 sq kilometres (including the Asian part of Russia)
POPULATION	731 million people
BIGGEST COUNTRY	Russia – 17,098,242 square kilometres
SMALLEST COUNTRY	Vatican City – total area 440,000 square metres
BIGGEST CITY	Moscow, Russia

Northern Europe

The countries here have long, cold winters. In Norway, Sweden and Finland most people live in towns and cities in the south, and near the coast. There are many trees in Northern Europe, and they are used for building, and for making paper and furniture. All the countries in this area are well known for their strong fishing industries.

3 City of ships

This old part of Copenhagen in Denmark used to be a busy port. But modern boats are too big to use it, so now it is a ship museum!

4 Fjords

There are lots of fjords along the coast of Norway. A fjord is a long valley with steep sides, and filled with sea water. Tourists travel from all over the world to see this lovely scenery.

1 The Ice Hotel

Every year in Sweden, people build an amazing hotel out of blocks of ice. Visitors sleep on ice beds covered in reindeer skins!

5 National dress

Each part of Norway has its own kind of traditional clothes, called 'bunad'. People wear their bunad for all kinds of celebrations.

2 Eurasian lynx

This wild cat lives in the forests of Estonia. Its feet have thick fur underneath to stop them sinking in the snow.

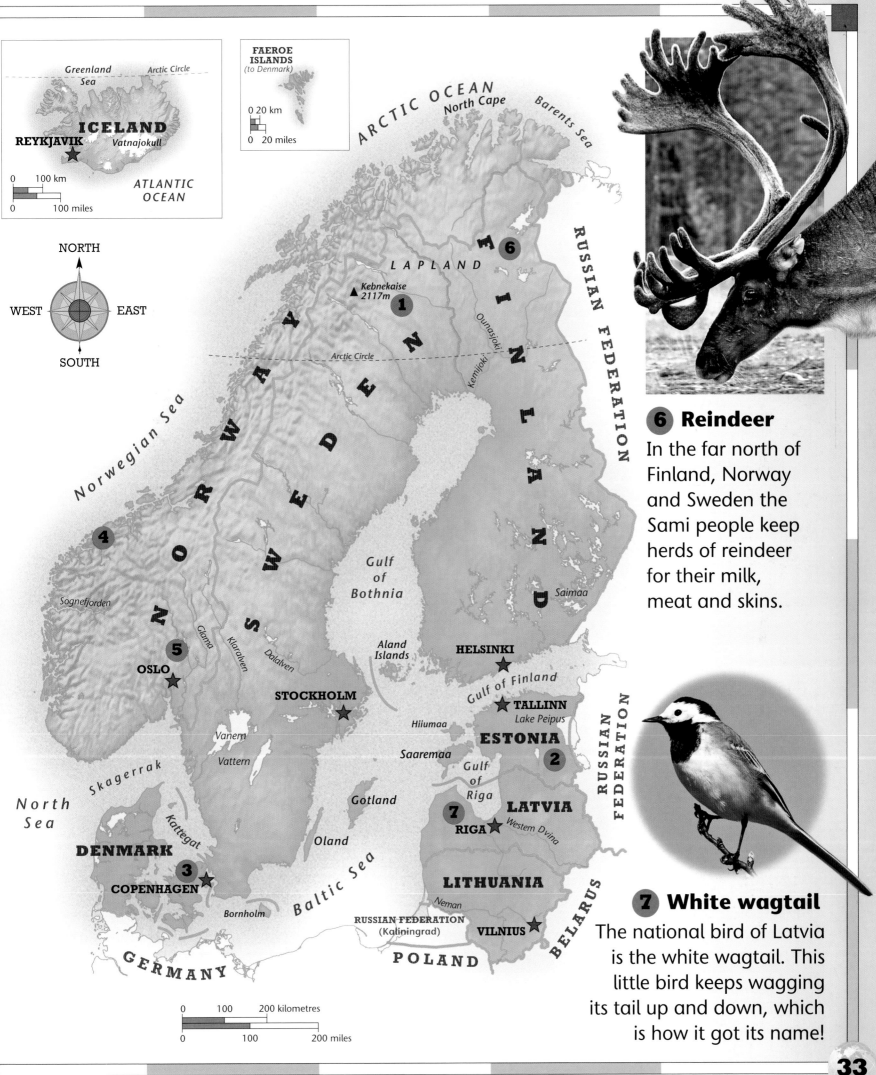

FAEROE ISLANDS
(to Denmark)

0 20 km
0 20 miles

Greenland Sea — *Arctic Circle*

ICELAND

REYKJAVIK ⭐ *Vatnajokull*

ATLANTIC OCEAN

0 100 km
0 100 miles

NORTH
WEST — EAST
SOUTH

ARCTIC OCEAN

North Cape   *Barents Sea*

L A P L A N D

RUSSIAN FEDERATION

▲ Kebnekaise
2117m **1**

6

Arctic Circle

N O R W A Y

S W E D E N

F I N L A N D

Ounasjoki

Kemijoki

Norwegian Sea

4

Sognefjorden

Gulf of Bothnia

Saimaa

Glama

5

OSLO ⭐

Klaralven

Dalalven

Aland Islands

HELSINKI ⭐

STOCKHOLM ⭐

Gulf of Finland

⭐ **TALLINN**

Lake Peipus

Hiiumaa

ESTONIA

2

Vanern

Vattern

Saaremaa

Gulf of Riga

North Sea

Skagerrak

Gotland

7
RIGA ⭐

LATVIA

Western Dvina

RUSSIAN FEDERATION

Kattegat

Oland

DENMARK

3
COPENHAGEN ⭐

Baltic Sea

Bornholm

LITHUANIA

Neman

RUSSIAN FEDERATION
(Kaliningrad)

VILNIUS ⭐

BELARUS

G E R M A N Y

P O L A N D

0 100 200 kilometres
0 100 200 miles

6 Reindeer

In the far north of Finland, Norway and Sweden the Sami people keep herds of reindeer for their milk, meat and skins.

7 White wagtail

The national bird of Latvia is the white wagtail. This little bird keeps wagging its tail up and down, which is how it got its name!

33

Western Europe

The land in Western Europe is good for farming and for growing many kinds of crops. It is quite rainy in the north and drier and hotter in the south. Most people live in large towns or cities. This area is popular with holidaymakers, and lots of tourists come to see the famous sights. It is easy to travel around, and nowhere is very far from the sea.

1 Big Ben

This tall clock tower is nicknamed 'Big Ben', after the huge bell inside it. It is part of a building in London called the Houses of Parliament, where politicians meet.

2 Spanish dancing

Spain is famous for its Flamenco dancers, who wear beautiful costumes. 'Flamenco' is the name for the traditional singing and dancing of gypsies from southern Spain.

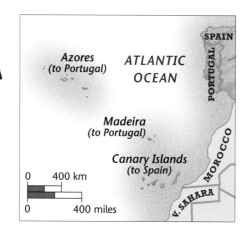

Shetland Islands

Orkney Islands

Outer Hebrides

3

SCOTLAND

NORTHERN IRELAND

UNITED KINGDOM

DUBLIN
IRELAND

ENGLAND

WALES

LONDON
Thames

English Channel

CHANNEL ISLANDS
(to UK)

ATLANTIC OCEAN

Bay of Biscay

Loire

PYR...

Ebro

Duero

SPAIN
MADRID

PORTUGAL

Tagus

Duero

LISBON

Guadiana

Guadalquivir

2

Gibraltar (to UK)

AFRICA

SPAIN

Azores
(to Portugal)

ATLANTIC OCEAN

PORTUGAL

Madeira
(to Portugal)

Canary Islands
(to Spain)

MOROCCO

W. SAHARA

0   400 km

0   400 miles

0   400 km

0   400 miles

3 Island birds

On the cliffs and islands around the coast of Scotland there are seabirds called puffins. They catch fish to eat by diving into the water.

4 Dutch tulips

Millions of tulips are grown in the flat fields of the Netherlands. The flowers and bulbs are sold all over the world. Many people visit here just to see the tulips!

5 Belgian chocolates

Belgium is famous for its chocolate. People have been making chocolates here for hundreds of years. Tourists enjoy buying and eating them!

6 Eiffel Tower

This is the most famous sight in France. The Eiffel Tower is 324 m tall, and weighs over 10,000 tons. It has six million visitors every year!

Central Europe

The north of Central Europe is quite flat and the land is good for farming. Most of the main industries are in the north. Central Europe has several long rivers. Many of the rivers are very wide, so big boats can travel by water to take all sorts of things from one place to another.

1 Beautiful Brandenburg Gate

This magnificent gate was one of the earliest gateways into the city of Berlin, in Germany. It has 12 tall columns, and on the top is a statue of Victoria, who was the Roman goddess of victory.

2 Skiing in the Alps

The Alps are one of the world's great mountain ranges. Every year, thousands of people enjoy skiing and walking in these beautiful mountains.

NORTH

WEST — EAST

SOUTH

0   100   200 kilometres

0   100   200 miles

THE WOW!

The Ancient Romans built roads, arches and aqueducts, and probably invented concrete. Many arches that they built thousands of years ago are still used today!

FACTOR

3 Bears in the woods

There are brown bears living wild in the forests of Slovenia. The Slovenian government is now trying to stop so many of these big mammals from being hunted and killed.

4 Pretty Prague

The beautiful old capital city of the Czech Republic is called Prague. It is also the country's largest city and is over 1,100 years old.

5 Carnival of Venice

Every Spring there is a famous carnival in Venice, in northern Italy. People dress up and wear fantastic masks.

6 Famous horses

Vienna, in Austria, is famous for its beautiful Lipizzaner stallions. These graceful horses are trained to do public performances.

Southeast Europe

There are many mountains in Southeast Europe, especially in the south. The south has hot, dry summers and mild winters. The north is warm in summer but it is very cold in winter. Farming is important all over most of Southeast Europe. The rich soil is perfect for growing crops such as grapes, tobacco, vegetables and wheat.

3 Sunflowers

The climate in Moldova is perfect for growing sunflowers! The flower seeds are pressed and their oil is exported around the world. Sunflower oil is used in cooking and it is also used as a fuel.

1 Greek buildings

On the islands of Greece lots of the houses and churches are painted white. The colour white reflects the light and heat from the sun. It helps to keep the buildings cool during the long, hot, dry summers.

2 Grey wolf

All dogs are related to grey wolves. Wolves used to live in the wild all over Europe. Now they are protected in some areas, and hunted in other areas. Sometimes wolves attack farm animals.

4 Mostar Bridge

Every year there is a high-diving competition off the bridge in the town of Mostar. This tall bridge was built in 1566 and is 20 m tall. It had to be re-built in 1999, after it was destroyed during a war.

5 Dracula's castle

Bran Castle in Romania is a national monument. Lots of tourists come to see it and it is nicknamed 'Dracula's castle'!

THE WOW!

Rose oil comes from the petals of millions of roses grown in Bulgaria. This beautifully scented oil is used in perfumes and it is sometimes worth more than gold!

FACTOR

LITHUANIA LATVIA

POLAND

SLOVAKIA

AUSTRIA

SLOVENIA

BELARUS

MINSK ★

Dnieper

Pripet

Pripet Marshes

RUSSIAN FEDERATION

7 ★ KIEV

U K R A I N E

Donets

Dnieper

CARPATHIAN MOUNTAINS

Dniester

Southern Bug

6 ★ BUDAPEST

Tisza

HUNGARY

Drava

★ ZAGREB

CROATIA

Sava

★ BELGRADE

BOSNIA & HERZEGOVINA

SARAJEVO ★

4

MONTENEGRO

PODGORICA ★

PRISTINA ★

★ KOSOVO

(only partially recognized)

Transylvania

ROMANIA 5

TRANSYLVANIAN ALPS

★ BUCHAREST

Danube

BULGARIA

BALKAN MOUNTAINS

★ SOFIA

RHODOPE

Musala 2925m ▲ MOUNTAINS

3

MOLDOVA

★ CHISINAU

Prut

BLACK SEA LOWLAND

Crimea

Sea of Azov

Black Sea

2

SKOPJE **MACEDONIA**

TIRANA ★

Lake Ohrid

Lake Prespa

ALBANIA

PINDOS MOUNTAINS

GREECE

Corfu

Ionian Sea

Aegean Sea

Lesbos

TURKEY

TURKEY

NORTH

WEST — EAST

SOUTH

★ ATHENS

Peloponnese

Mediterranean Sea

1

Sea of Crete

Rhodes

Crete

0   100   200 kilometres

0   100   200 miles

6 Peppers

In Hungary peppers stuffed with rice, meat and vegetables are a popular meal. Peppers are also used to make a spice called paprika.

7 Folk costumes

There are lots of different folk costumes in Ukraine. The women's and children's are usually brighter than the men's. Children sometimes wear pretty flowers, too.

Russian Federation

Russia is the biggest country in the world. Part of it is in Europe and part of it is in Asia. A lot of Russia is covered in trees, and in the north the ground is snowy and frozen all year. Further south, the climate is milder. Russia has plenty of oil and natural gas, with large areas of rich soil, which are perfect for farming.

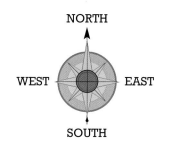

1 The Kremlin in Moscow

This church is part of the Kremlin in Moscow. The word 'kremlin' means a fortress or a castle. The Kremlin is the official home of the President of Russia. It has four palaces and four cathedrals.

2 Corsac fox

These foxes live on the open plains and mountainous areas of northern Russia. They often have several fox dens with lots of connecting holes!

3 Trans-Siberian Railway

To travel all the way across Russia on the Trans-Siberian Railway takes seven days. It goes through eight time zones!

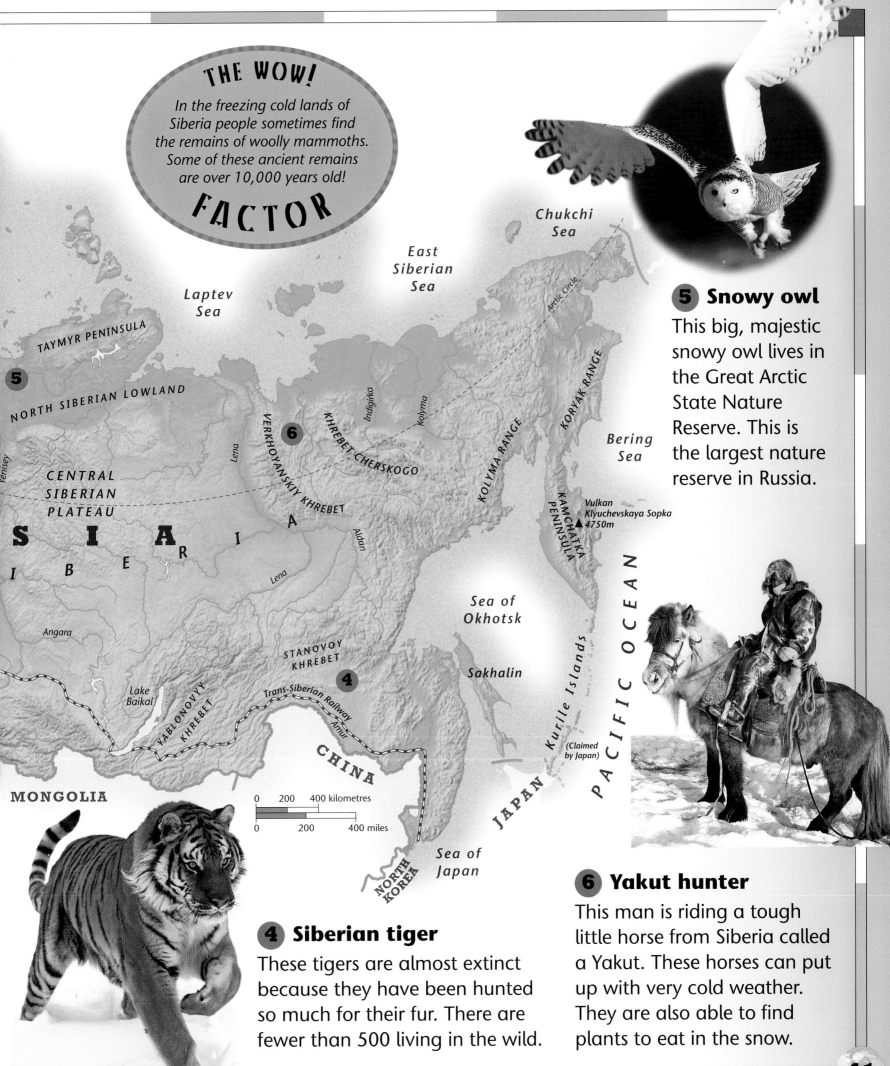

Chukchi Sea

East Siberian Sea

Laptev Sea

TAYMYR PENINSULA

5

NORTH SIBERIAN LOWLAND

Yenisey

CENTRAL SIBERIAN PLATEAU

Lena

6

VERKHOYANSKIY KHREBET

KHREBET CHERSKOGO

Indigirka

Kolyma

Arctic Circle

KOLYMA RANGE

KORYAK RANGE

Bering Sea

S I B E R I A

Aldan

Lena

Angara

Vulkan Klyuchevskaya Sopka ▲ 4750m

KAMCHATKA PENINSULA

STANOVOY KHREBET

Sea of Okhotsk

P A C I F I C   O C E A N

Lake Baikal

YABLONOVY KHREBET

Trans-Siberian Railway

4

Amur

Sakhalin

Kurile Islands

MONGOLIA

CHINA

0   200   400 kilometres

0   200   400 miles

(Claimed by Japan)

JAPAN

Sea of Japan

NORTH KOREA

5 Snowy owl

This big, majestic snowy owl lives in the Great Arctic State Nature Reserve. This is the largest nature reserve in Russia.

6 Yakut hunter

This man is riding a tough little horse from Siberia called a Yakut. These horses can put up with very cold weather. They are also able to find plants to eat in the snow.

4 Siberian tiger

These tigers are almost extinct because they have been hunted so much for their fur. There are fewer than 500 living in the wild.

Europe country facts

There are 45 countries in Europe and more than 230 languages. The two languages used most often are English and German. There are more than 20 different sorts of currency, and 23 countries are using the euro. You can see all of Europe's flags on these pages.

Iceland
Capital City Reykjavik
Population 308,910
Area 103,000 sq km
Main languages Icelandic
Money 1 Icelandic krona = 100 aurar

Norway
Capital City Oslo
Population 4,676,305
Area 323,802 sq km
Main languages Norwegian
Money 1 Norwegian krone = 100 ore

Denmark
Capital City Copenhagen
Population 5,515,575
Area 43,094 sq km
Main languages Danish
Money 1 Danish krone = 100 ore

Sweden
Capital City Stockholm
Population 9,074,055
Area 450,295 sq km
Main languages Swedish
Money 1 Swedish krona = 100 ore

Finland
Capital City Helsinki
Population 5,255,068
Area 338,145 sq km
Main languages Finnish and Swedish
Money 1 euro = 100 cents

Russia
Capital City Moscow
Population 139,390,205
Area 17,098,242 sq km
Main languages Russian
Money 1 ruble = 100 kopecs

Belarus
Capital City Minsk
Population 9,612,632
Area 207,600 sq km
Main languages Belarusian and Russian
Money 1 Belarusian ruble = 100 kapeykas

Ireland
Capital City Dublin
Population 4,622,917
Area 70,273 sq km
Main languages English and Irish
Money 1 euro = 100 cents

United Kingdom
Capital City London
Population 62,348,447
Area 243,610 sq km
Main languages English, Welsh
Money 1 pound sterling = 100 pennies

Netherlands
Capital Cities Amsterdam and The Hague
Population 16,783,092
Area 41,543 sq km
Main languages Dutch
Money 1 euro = 100 cents

Belgium
Capital City Brussels
Population 10,423,493
Area 30,528 sq km
Main languages Dutch, French and German
Money 1 euro = 100 cents

Luxembourg
Capital City Luxembourg
Population 497,538
Area 2,586 sq km
Main languages German, French and Luxembourgish
Money 1 euro = 100 cents

Visit London!

The capital of the United Kingdom is London. This is the most visited city in the world. London is famous for its theatres, museums, art, business and fashion. One of London's famous sights is this giant wheel, called the London Eye.

Germany
Capital City Berlin
Population 82,282,988
Area 357,022 sq km
Main languages German
Money 1 euro = 100 cents

Poland
Capital City Warsaw
Population 38,463,689
Area 312,685 sq km
Main languages Polish
Money 1 zloty = 100 groszy

Lithuania
Capital City Vilnius
Population 3,545,319
Area 65,300 sq km
Main languages Lithuanian,
Polish and Russian
Money 1 Lithuanian litas =
100 centu

Latvia
Capital City Riga
Population 2,217,969
Area 64,589 sq km
Main languages Latvian
and Russian
Money 1 Latvian lats =
100 santimi

Estonia
Capital City Tallinn
Population 1,291,170
Area 45,228 sq km
Main languages Estonian
and Russian
Money 1 Euro = 100 cents

France

France
Capital City Paris
Population 64,768,389
Area 643,427 sq km
Main languages French
Money 1 euro = 100 cents

Switzerland
Capital City Bern
Population 7,623,438
Area 41,277 sq km
Main languages German,
French, Italian and Romansch
Money 1 Swiss franc =
100 centimes

Liechtenstein
Capital City Vaduz
Population 35,002
Area 160 sq km
Main languages German
and Alemannic
Money 1 Swiss franc =
100 centimes

Austria
Capital City Vienna
Population 8,214,160
Area 83,871 sq km
Main languages German
Money 1 euro = 100 cents

Czech Republic
Capital City Prague
Population 10,201,717
Area 78,867 sq km
Main languages Czech
Money 1 koruna = 100 haleru

Hungary
Capital City Budapest
Population 9,992,339
Area 93,028 sq km
Main languages Hungarian
Money 1 forint = 100 filler

The Grand Duchy

Luxembourg is one of the smallest countries
in the world, and one of the richest in Europe.
The official name for Luxembourg is the Grand
Duchy of Luxembourg. It is ruled by a Grand
Duke and is the only Grand Duchy in the world!

Slovakia
Capital City Bratislava
Population 5,470,306
Area 49,035 sq km
Main languages Slovak
Money 1 euro = 100 cents

Romania
Capital City Bucharest
Population 21,959,278
Area 238,391sq km
Main languages Romanian
Money 1 Romanian leu =
100 bani

Moldova
Capital City Chisinau
Population 4,317,483
Area 33,851 sq km
Main languages Moldovan,
Russian and Gagauz
Money 1 Moldovian leu =
100 bani

Ukraine
Capital City Kiev
Population 45,415,596
Area 603,550 sq km
Main languages Ukranian
and Russian
Money 1 hryvnia = 100 kopiyok

Main languages Bosnian, Serbian, Croatian
Money 1 convertible mark = 100 feninga

Bulgaria
Capital City Sofia
Population 7,148,785
Area 110,879 sq km
Main languages Bulgarian
Money 1 lev = 100 stotinki

Andorra
Capital City Andorra La Vella
Population 84,525
Area 468 sq km
Main languages Spanish, French, Portuguese
Money 1 euro = 100 cents

Small and wealthy

The rich country of Monaco is so tiny that you can walk from one side of it to the other side in half an hour, but this is also Europe's most crowded country. More people live here per square kilometre than anywhere else in Europe.

Vatican City
Capital City Vatican City
Population 826
Area 0.44 sq km
Main languages Italian
Money 1 euro = 100 cents

Bosnia and Herzegovina
Capital City Sarajevo
Population 4,621,598
Area 51,197 sq km

Montenegro
Capital City Podgorica
Population 666,730
Area 13,812
Main languages Serbian, Montenegrin
Money 1 euro = 100 cents

Monaco
Capital City Monaco-Ville
Population 30,586
Area 2 sq km
Main languages French
Money 1 euro = 100 cents

San Marino
Capital City San Marino
Population 31,477
Area 61 sq km
Main languages Italian
Money 1 euro = 100 cents

Slovenia
Capital City Ljubljana
Population 2,003,136
Area 20,273 sq km
Main languages Slovenian
Money 1 euro = 100 cents

Croatia
Capital City Zagreb
Population 4,486,881
Area 56,594 sq km
Main languages Croatian
Money 1 kuna = 100 lipa

Serbia
Capital City Belgrade
Population 7,344,847
Area 77,474 sq km
Main languages Serbian
Money Serbian dinar
(Dinars are not divided into smaller units.)

Kosovo
Capital City Pristina
Population 1,815,048
Area 10,887 sq km
Main languages Albanian, Serbian
Money 1 euro = 100 cents

Newest capital city

Europe's newest capital is Pristina, in Kosovo. Its National Library is an amazing building covered in a big metal net. It represents the brain and learning

Macedonia
Capital City Skopje
Population 2,072,086
Area 25,713
Main languages Macedonian
Money 1 Macedonian denar =
100 deni

Spain
Capital City Madrid
Population 46,505,963
Area 505,370 sq km
Main languages Spanish,
Catalan, Galician, Basque
Money 1 euro = 100 cents

Italy
Capital City Rome
Population 58,090,681
Area 301,340 sq km
Main languages Italian
Money 1 euro = 100 cents

Albania
Capital City Tirana
Population 2,986,952

Area 28,748 sq km
Main languages Albanian
Money 1 lek = 100 qindark
(Lek are no longer divided
into smaller units.)

Portugal
Capital City Lisbon
Population 10,735,765
Area 92,090 sq km
Main languages Portuguese,
Mirandese
Money 1 euro = 100 cents

Malta
Capital City Valletta
Population 406,771
Area 316 sq km
Main languages Maltese,
English
Money 1 euro = 100 cents

Greece
Capital City Athens
Population 10,749,943
Area 131,957 sq km
Main languages Greek
Money 1 euro = 100 cents

Where are you from?

Here are some of the European national car stickers. Everyone who drives their car outside their own country has to put a sticker on the back bumper of the car. Or, they must have a number plate that shows which country they are from.

☆ The fronts of all the euro coins are the same for every country that uses the euro. This is the front of a two euro coin.

☆ The designs on the backs of euro coins are usually different for each country. Here are the backs of the two euro coins from six countries in Europe.

TELL US ABOUT THE EURO!

☆ Euro coins are designed so that people can recognise which coins they have just by touching them. Each euro coin is a different size and weight and each has a special, and different, edge.

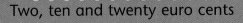

Two, ten and twenty euro cents

Malta

Germany

France

Italy

Netherlands

Cyprus

Asia

This is the world's biggest continent, with 48 countries. The largest country is Russia, then China. The smallest is the Republic of Maldives. More people live in Asia than in any other continent. There are over 1,500 languages and lots of religions and cultures.

Biggest city

Mumbai, in India, is the biggest city in Asia. This 'mega city' is home to over 14 million people. They earn much more here than people in the rest of India.

Smallest country

Asia's smallest country is made up of a group of beautiful islands in the Indian Ocean. They are called the Maldives. These tiny islands are actually the tops of a gigantic underwater mountain range!

NORTH

WEST · EAST

SOUTH

R

KAZAKHSTAN

Black Sea

GEORGIA
ARMENIA
TURKEY
AZERBAIJAN
AZER.
UZBEKISTAN
TURKMENISTAN
KYRGYZSTAN
TAJIKISTAN
AFGHANISTAN

CYPRUS
LEBANON
ISRAEL
SYRIA
IRAQ
JORDAN
IRAN
PAKISTAN
NEPAL
BHUTA

KUWAIT
BAHRAIN
QATAR
U.A.E
BANGLADESH

Red Sea

SAUDI ARABIA
OMAN
Arabian Sea
INDIA
Bay of Benga

YEMEN

List of Abbreviations

U.A.E. United Arab Emirates

SRI LANKA

MALDIVES

INDIAN OCEAN

ARCTIC OCEAN

RUSSIA

Bering Sea

Sea of Okhotsk

MONGOLIA

NORTH KOREA

SOUTH KOREA

JAPAN

CHINA

East China Sea

TAIWAN

(MYANMAR)

THAILAND

LAOS

VIETNAM

CAMBODIA

South China Sea

PHILIPPINES

PACIFIC OCEAN

BRUNEI

MALAYSIA

SINGAPORE

INDONESIA

TIMOR LESTE

Volcanic islands

Indonesia is made up of 17,508 islands. It is one of the most volcanic places on earth, with over 150 active volcanoes. This volcano is called Anak Krakatoa.

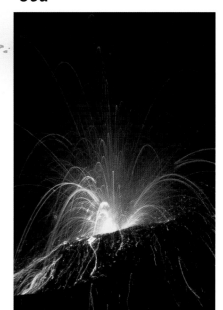

ABOUT ASIA

NUMBER OF COUNTRIES	48
SIZE	World's largest continent
TOTAL AREA	44,579,000 sq kilometres (including the Asian part of Russia)
POPULATION	3.9 billion people
BIGGEST COUNTRY	Russia – 17,098,242 square kilometres
SMALLEST COUNTRY	Maldives – total area 298 square kilometres
BIGGEST CITY	Mumbai (Bombay), India

Southwest Asia

This huge area of land has lots of dry deserts and high mountains. The hot climate and the dry land make farming difficult, but people have lived here for over 7,000 years. Now most people live close to the coast, especially by the Mediterranean Sea. Many countries have become very rich because of oil.

BULGARIA

Istanbu

GREECE

TURKISH REPUBLIC
NORTHERN CYPR
(recognized only by Turk

Med

1 A city of two halves

Istanbul is the only city in the world that is in two continents. One half of this city is in Europe, and the other half is in Asia!

```
0        200      400 kilometres
0            200        400 miles
```

2 Antelopes in trouble

This antelope is an ibex. They used to live all over the south of Southwest Asia. Now there are only about 1,200 in the wild. Ibexes have been hunted for their skin, meat and horns.

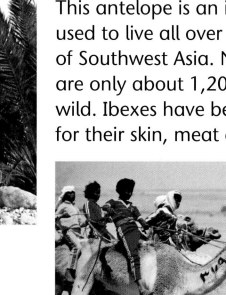

3 Ancient city

In Jordan, hidden down a passageway between tall cliffs, there are ruins of an ancient city called Petra. Many of its beautiful buildings are carved out of rock. Every year thousands of tourists come to see Petra.

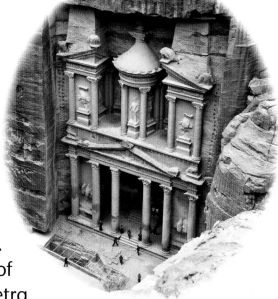

4 Camel racing

This camel race at Riyadh, in Saudi Arabia, has 20,000 spectators and more than 2,000 camels. Most of the camels are ridden by boys. The winning camels are worth millions of US dollars

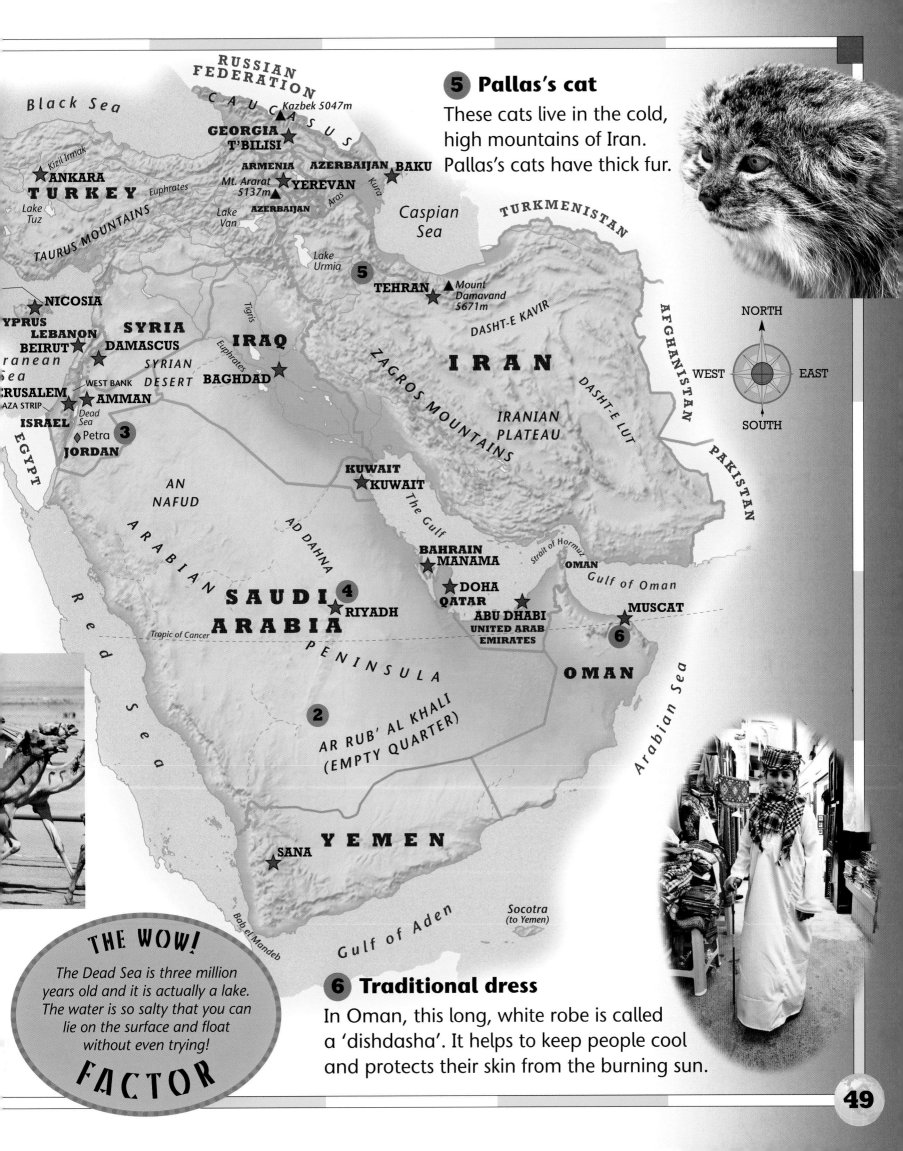

RUSSIAN FEDERATION

Black Sea

C A U C A S U S

Kazbek 5047m ▲

Kizil Irmak

★ ANKARA

GEORGIA
★ T'BILISI

TURKEY

Euphrates

ARMENIA **AZERBAIJAN** ★ **BAKU**

Mt. Ararat 5137m ▲ ★ YEREVAN

Lake Van

Lake Tuz

TAURUS MOUNTAINS

AZERBAIJAN

Aras

Kura

Lake Urmia

TURKMENISTAN

Caspian Sea

★ NICOSIA

YPRUS

LEBANON

BEIRUT ★

Tigris

⑤ TEHRAN ★ ▲ Mount Damavand 5671m

DASHT-E KAVIR

SYRIA

DAMASCUS ★

IRAQ

SYRIAN DESERT

Euphrates

I R A N

ZAGROS MOUNTAINS

AFGHANISTAN

ranean Sea

RUSALEM ★

WEST BANK

AZA STRIP

★ AMMAN

BAGHDAD ★

IRANIAN PLATEAU

DASHT-E LUT

ISRAEL

Dead Sea

◆ Petra

③

PAKISTAN

EGYPT

JORDAN

AN NAFUD

KUWAIT
★ KUWAIT

The Gulf

NORTH

WEST ✦ EAST

SOUTH

A R A B I A N

AD DAHNA

Red Sea

SAUDI ④
ARABIA ★ RIYADH

Tropic of Cancer

BAHRAIN
MANAMA ★

Strait of Hormuz

★ DOHA
QATAR

★
ABU DHABI
UNITED ARAB EMIRATES

OMAN

Gulf of Oman

★ MUSCAT

⑥

P E N I N S U L A

②

AR RUB' AL KHALI
(EMPTY QUARTER)

O M A N

Arabian Sea

Y E M E N

★ SANA

Bab el Mandeb

Gulf of Aden

Socotra
(to Yemen)

⑤ Pallas's cat

These cats live in the cold, high mountains of Iran. Pallas's cats have thick fur.

⑥ Traditional dress

In Oman, this long, white robe is called a 'dishdasha'. It helps to keep people cool and protects their skin from the burning sun.

THE WOW!

The Dead Sea is three million years old and it is actually a lake. The water is so salty that you can lie on the surface and float without even trying!

FACTOR

Central Asia

The land in Central Asia is cut off from the sea and it has many mountains and deserts. Kazakhstan has big open plains, which are good for farming. It hardly ever rains and winters are cold and snowy. The summers can be hot. There are only a few towns, and most people live in villages.

1 Common hamster

This little mammal is a type of rodent. Common hamsters live in the wild all over Kazakhstan and Russia. Hamsters are also popular in Europe as pets!

2 Rocky lands

Apart from the huge plains and steppes of Kazakhstan, large parts of Central Asia are rocky and mountainous, such as Uzbekistan. The rugged scenery here is very beautiful.

RUSSIAN FEDERATION

1

Caspian Depressio

Caspian Sea

IRAN

3 Afghan hound

These large dogs were first bred in Afghanistan. Afghan hounds were used as hunting dogs and as farm dogs, to help the farmers herd their sheep.

4 Ancient horse breed

The Akhal-Teke is one of the world's oldest breeds of horse. It comes from Turkmenistan and is the national emblem of that country. These horses are fast and strong, and are able to survive bitterly cold winters.

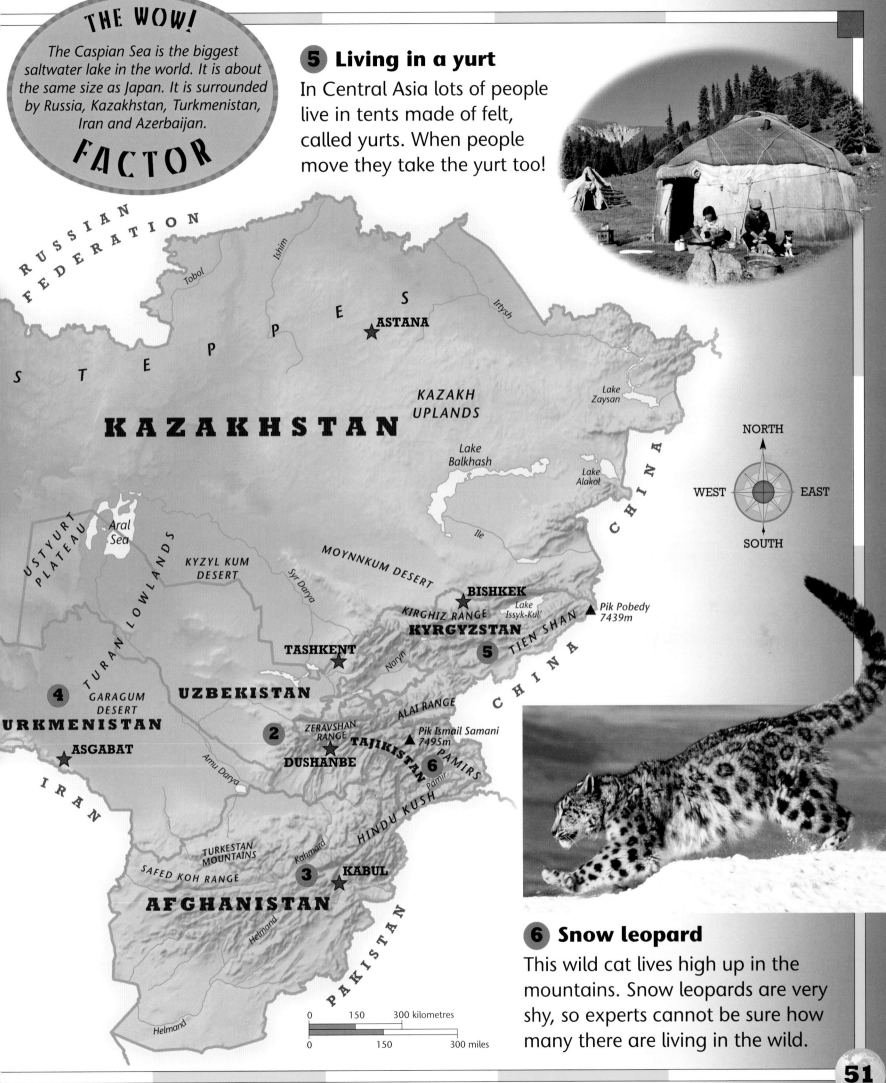

5 Living in a yurt

In Central Asia lots of people live in tents made of felt, called yurts. When people move they take the yurt too!

RUSSIAN FEDERATION

Tobol

Ishim

Tobol

Irtysh

STEPPES

★ ASTANA

KAZAKH UPLANDS

Lake Zaysan

KAZAKHSTAN

Lake Balkhash

Lake Alakol

CHINA

NORTH

WEST   EAST

SOUTH

USTYURT PLATEAU

Aral Sea

KYZYL KUM DESERT

Syr Darya

MOYNNKUM DESERT

Ile

TURAN LOWLANDS

4

GARAGUM DESERT

UZBEKISTAN

TASHKENT ★

BISHKEK ★

KIRGHIZ RANGE

Lake Issyk-Kul'

KYRGYZSTAN

5 TIEN SHAN

Pik Pobedy 7439m ▲

CHINA

Naryn

ALAI RANGE

URKMENISTAN

ASGABAT ★

2 ZERAVSHAN RANGE

Amu Darya

DUSHANBE ★

TAJIKISTAN

Pik Ismail Samani 7495m ▲

6 PAMIRS

Pamir

IRAN

HINDU KUSH

TURKESTAN MOUNTAINS

Kahmard

SAFED KOH RANGE

3 KABUL ★

AFGHANISTAN

Helmand

Helmand

PAKISTAN

0   150   300 kilometres

0   150   300 miles

6 Snow leopard

This wild cat lives high up in the mountains. Snow leopards are very shy, so experts cannot be sure how many there are living in the wild.

South Asia

This part of the world is also known as the Indian subcontinent. It is separated from China by high, snowy mountains called the Himalayas. In the south are hot, tropical rainforests and in the west are huge areas of desert. Most people are farmers, but they only grow enough for their families to eat.

1 Taj Mahal

This beautiful building in Agra, India, is called the Taj Mahal. The emperor Shah Jahan had it built in 1648 in memory of his wife, Mumtaz Mahal.

2 At the border

Every evening, at the border between India and Pakistan, guards march up and down. They kick their legs up high to show the soles of their boots to each other. This is rude in both of their countries!

3 Colourful festival

At the beginning of the ancient Indian festival of Holi there is a procession of animals. The most beautifully decorated elephant is given a prize!

4 Indian rhinoceros

These large mammals live close to rivers in Nepal and northeast India. They like to stand in water to keep cool, and they feed on grass.

5 River Ganges

The biggest river in India is the River Ganges. It is holy to Hindu people. They come to bathe in it, and worship it as the god 'Ganga'.

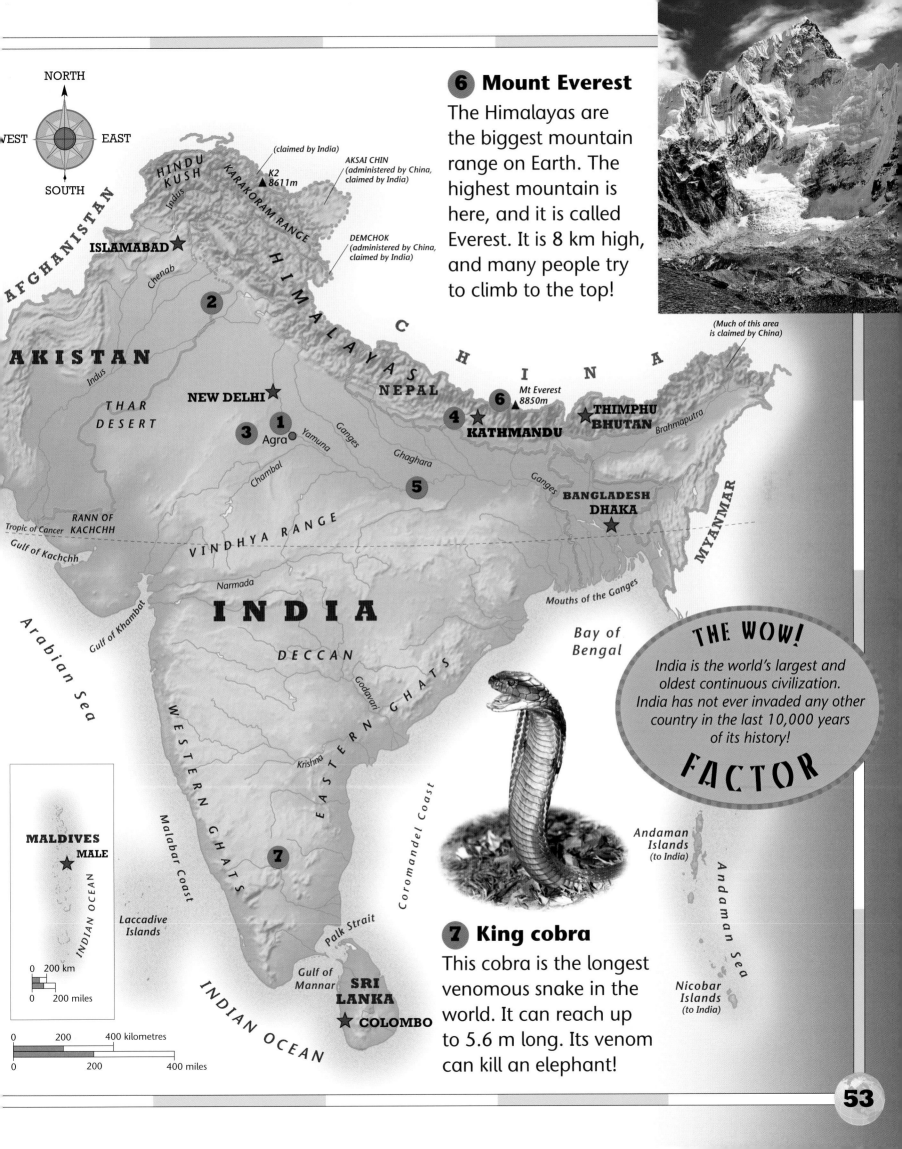

NORTH

WEST — EAST

SOUTH

AFGHANISTAN

HINDU KUSH

KARAKORAM RANGE

K2
▲ 8611m

(claimed by India)

AKSAI CHIN
(administered by China,
claimed by India)

DEMCHOK
(administered by China,
claimed by India)

ISLAMABAD ★

Indus

Chenab

HIMALAYAS

C H I N A

AKISTAN

Indus

THAR
DESERT

NEW DELHI ★

NEPAL

(Much of this area
is claimed by China)

Mt Everest
8850m
▲

3   1

Agra ●   Yamuna

Ganges

Ghaghara

4 ★

6

KATHMANDU

★ THIMPHU
BHUTAN

Brahmaputra

2

Chambal

5

Ganges

BANGLADESH
DHAKA

RANN OF
KACHCHH

Tropic of Cancer

Gulf of Kachchh

VINDHYA RANGE

Narmada

★

MYANMAR

INDIA

DECCAN

Mouths of the Ganges

Bay of
Bengal

Arabian Sea

Gulf of Khambat

WESTERN GHATS

EASTERN GHATS

Godavari

Krishna

Coromandel Coast

Andaman Islands
(to India)

Malabar Coast

MALDIVES
★ MALE

INDIAN OCEAN

Laccadive
Islands

0   200 km

0   200 miles

Palk Strait

Gulf of
Mannar

SRI
LANKA

★ COLOMBO

Andaman Sea

Nicobar
Islands
(to India)

INDIAN OCEAN

0   200   400 kilometres

0   200   400 miles

6 Mount Everest

The Himalayas are the biggest mountain range on Earth. The highest mountain is here, and it is called Everest. It is 8 km high, and many people try to climb to the top!

THE WOW!

India is the world's largest and oldest continuous civilization. India has not ever invaded any other country in the last 10,000 years of its history!

FACTOR

7 King cobra

This cobra is the longest venomous snake in the world. It can reach up to 5.6 m long. Its venom can kill an elephant!

East Asia

In East Asia there are many high mountains, deserts and flat open plains, called steppes. Most of the people live in the east, where it is flatter and the climate is warmer.

1 Giant panda

These big bears live in a few mountain ranges in China. They spend most of their day eating bamboo!

2 Gigantic Gobi

The Gobi is one of the world's largest deserts. The name 'Gobi' means desert in Mongolian. It is huge, cold, dry and rocky. Experts find lots of fossils here, including fossilized dinosaur eggs!

KAZAKHSTAN

KYRGYZSTAN

TAJIKISTAN

PAKISTAN

ALTAI MOUNTAINS

TIEN SHAN

TARIM BASIN

(Claimed by India)

K2
▲8611m

TAKLA MAKAN DESERT

KUNLUN MOUNTAINS

ALTUN SHAN

QILIAN SHA

QAIDAM BASIN

Aksai Chin
(Administered by China,
claimed by India)

Demchok
(Administered by China,
claimed by India)

PLATEAU OF TIBET

C   H

INDIA

HIMALAYAS

NEPAL

Salween

Tibet

Brahmaputra

Mt Everest
8850m

BHUTAN

INDIA

MYANMAR

LA

Mekong

NORTH

WEST   EAST

SOUTH

3 Dragon dance

In China, people believe that dragons bring good luck. At Chinese New Year people do dances using big paper dragons.

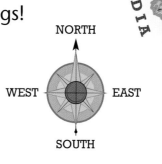

4 Eagle hunter

In western Mongolia people train eagles to hunt foxes, rabbits and even wolves. People in Mongolia have hunted with eagles for thousands of years.

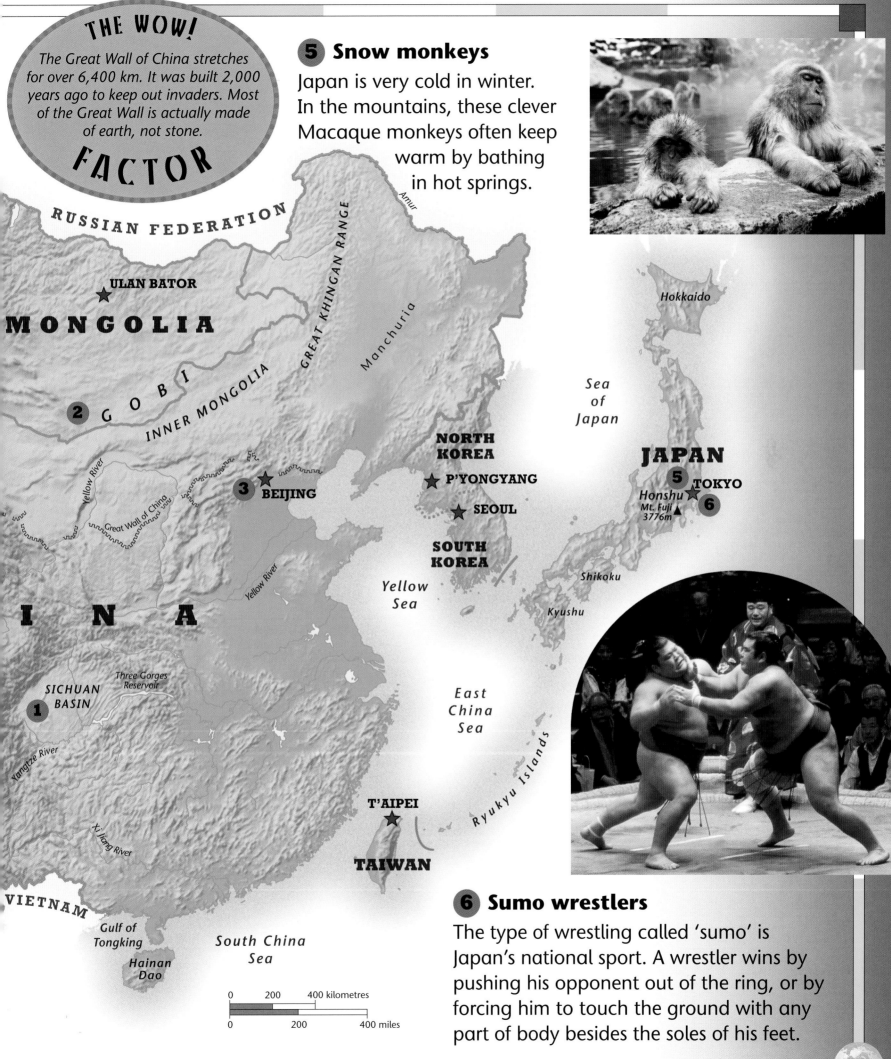

5 Snow monkeys

Japan is very cold in winter. In the mountains, these clever Macaque monkeys often keep warm by bathing in hot springs.

RUSSIAN FEDERATION

Amur

ULAN BATOR ★

GREAT KHINGAN RANGE

Manchuria

Hokkaido

MONGOLIA

② *G O B I*

INNER MONGOLIA

Sea of Japan

Yellow River

NORTH KOREA

★ **P'YONGYANG**

JAPAN

⑤ ★ **TOKYO**

③ ★ **BEIJING**

Honshu ★ ⑥

Mt. Fuji 3776m ▲

Great Wall of China

★ **SEOUL**

I N A

Yellow River

SOUTH KOREA

Shikoku

Yellow Sea

Kyushu

SICHUAN BASIN

① *Three Gorges Reservoir*

East China Sea

Yangtze River

Ryukyu Islands

Xi Jiang River

T'AIPEI

★

TAIWAN

VIETNAM

Gulf of Tongking

South China Sea

Hainan Dao

| 0 | 200 | 400 kilometres |
| 0 | 200 | 400 miles |

6 Sumo wrestlers

The type of wrestling called 'sumo' is Japan's national sport. A wrestler wins by pushing his opponent out of the ring, or by forcing him to touch the ground with any part of body besides the soles of his feet.

55

Southeast Asia

Most of Southeast Asia is covered in tropical forests and mountains. For half of the year it is rainy and for half of the year it is dry. This is called a monsoon climate. The people live mainly along the river valleys and near the coast. Southeast Asia has many languages, religions and cultures.

1 Floating market

In the city of Bangkok, in Thailand, people sell their fruit and vegetables from long, narrow boats on the canals. This colourful floating market is famous.

2 Myanmar's lost city

A thousand years ago this was a busy city called Bagan. Then the city was left empty for hundreds of years. When it was found again, a forest had grown all over it!

3 Sumatran tiger

These are the world's smallest tigers. There are less than 300 left in the wild and they live on the island of Sumatra. All tigers are endangered.

5 Orang-utan

These apes live in the forests of Borneo. They spend most of the day looking for food such as leaves, shoots, eggs and insects. They are very endangered.

4 Growing rice

People grow rice all over Asia, and it is one of the most important foods in the world. Billions of people eat rice as their main diet.

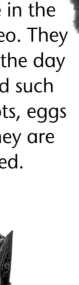

6 Carved masks

In Indonesia actors and dancers wear masks like this one. Carving masks out of wood is an ancient craft.

7 Mega flower

The world's biggest flowers are the Rafflesias in Asia. Some grow to 50 cm across. These flowers smell like rotting meat!

Luzon

MANILA ★

Philippine Sea

PHILIPPINES

Sulu Sea

Mindanao

BANDAR SERI BEGAWAN ★

BRUNEI

Mount Kinabalu ▲ 4101m

⑤

Celebes Sea

S I A

Borneo

Equator

PACIFIC OCEAN

Molucca Sea

Sulawesi

Papua

PAPUA NEW GUINEA

S u n d a   I s l a n d s

D   **O**   **N**   **E**   **S**   **I**   **A**

▲ *Puncak Jaya 4884m*

Java Sea

Banda Sea

Flores Sea

Bali   **L e s s e r   S u n d a   I s l a n d s**

⑥   *Flores*

Komodo

★ **DILI**

TIMOR LESTE

Timor

Timor Sea

Arafura Sea

| 0 | 250 | 500 kilometres |
| 0 | 250 | 500 miles |

THE WOW!

On the island of Komodo are giant lizards called Komodo dragons. They are the world's biggest lizards and are over 3 m long. They are fierce and have poisonous saliva!

FACTOR

Asia country facts

There are 48 countries in Asia and more than 1,500 languages are spoken here. Chinese Mandarin, Hindi, Bengali and English are the most widely used languages. There are 48 currencies being used in Asia, including the euro and the US dollar.

Kazakhstan
Capital City Astana
Population 15,460,484
Area 2,724,900 sq km
Main languages Kazakh, Russian
Money 1 Kazakh tenge = 100 tiyn

Uzbekistan
Capital City Tashkent (Toshkent)
Population 27,865,738
Area 447,400 sq km
Main languages Uzbek, Russian, Tajik
Money 1 Uzbek som = 100 tiyins

Cyprus
Capital City Nicosia (Lefkosia)
Population 1,102,677
Area 9,251 sq km
Main languages Greek, Turkish
Money 1 euro = 100 cents

Turkey
Capital City Ankara
Population 77,804,122
Area 783,562 sq km
Main languages Turkish
Money 1 Turkish lira = 100 kuru

Georgia
Capital City T'bilisi
Population 4,600,825
Area 69,700 sq km
Main languages Georgian
Money 1 lari = 100 tetri

Kyrgyzstan
Capital City Bishkek
Population 5,508,626
Area 199,951 sq km
Main languages Kyrgyz, Russian
Money 1 som = 100 tiyins

Lebanon
Capital City Beirut
Population 4,125,247
Area 10,400 sq km
Main languages Arabic
Money 1 Lebanese pound (or lira) = 100 piastres

Syria
Capital City Damascus
Population 22,198,110
Area 185,180 sq km
Main languages Arabic
Money 1 Syrian pound = 100 piastres

Holy city

The capital city of Israel is Jerusalem. For the three major religions – Judaism, Islam and Christianity – this is the holiest city in the world. Many people believe that it is the place where both Mohammed and Jesus rose into Heaven.

Armenia
Capital City Yerevan
Population 2,966,802
Area 29,743 sq km
Main languages Armenian, Russian
Money 1 dram = 100 lumas

Turkmenistan
Capital City Ashgabat (Ashkhabad)
Population 4,940,916
Area 488,100 sq km
Main languages Turkmen, Russian
Money 1 Turkmen manat = 100 tenge

Israel
Capital City Jerusalem
Population 7,353,985
Area 22,072 sq km
Main languages Hebrew, Arabic
Money 1 new Israeli shekel = 100 new agorot

Iraq
Capital City Baghdad
Population 29,671,605
Area 438,317 sq km
Main languages Arabic, Kurdish
Money 1 Iraqi dinar = 1,000 fils

Room to roam

The country of Mongolia is enormous but very few people live here. There are only about three million people in the whole country. There is hardly any farmland, and large areas of the country are covered by mountains, grassy plains called steppes, and the Gobi – a big, cold desert.

Azerbaijan
Capital City Baku (Baki, Baky)
Population 8,303,512
Area 86,600 sq km
Main languages Azeri, Russian
Money 1 manat = 100 qapik

Tajikistan
Capital City Dushanbe
Population 7,487,489
Area 143,100 sq km
Main languages Tajik, Uzbek, Russian
Money 1 Tajik somoni = 100 dirams

Jordan
Capital City Amman
Population 6,407,085
Area 89,342 sq km
Main languages Arabic
Money 1 Jordan dinar = 1,000 fils

Kuwait
Capital City Kuwait City
Population 2,789,132
Area 17,818 sq km
Main languages Arabic
Money 1 dinar = 1,000 fils

Iran
Capital City Tehran
Population 76,923,300
Area 1,648,195 sq km
Main languages Persian
Money 10 Iranian rials = 1 toman

Afghanistan
Capital City Kabul
Population 29,121,286

Area 652,230 sq km
Main languages Pashto, Dari (Persian)
Money 1 Afghani = 100 puls

Bhutan
Capital City Thimphu
Population 699,847
Area 38,394 sq km
Main languages Dzongkha
Money 1 ngultrum = 100 chetrum

Mongolia
Capital City Ulaanbaatar
Population 3,086,918
Area 1,564,116 sq km
Main languages Mongolian
Money 1 togrog (tugrik) = 100 mongos

China
Capital City Beijing
Population 1,330,141,295
Area 9,596,961 sq km
Main languages Mandarin Chinese
Money 1 renminbi (yuan) = 10 jiao = 100 fen

MODERN CHINA

★ After communist Chairman Mao died in 1976 the Chinese government began to allow people to farm, and buy and sell things for themselves. Now China exports all sorts of things, including toys, clothes, books and computers, to other places in the world. Many countries spend lots of money on Chinese goods. This has made China become a very rich country.

Shanghai is the fastest growing city in China.

Japan's capital

The richest nation in Asia is Japan. Tokyo is the largest city, and it is the capital of Japan. Japan's government is based in Tokyo, and the Imperial Palace is here, too. This is the home of the Emperor of Japan.

Taiwan
Capital City Taipei
Population 23,142,360
Area 35,980 sq km
Main languages Mandarin Chinese, Min Nan Chinese (Taiwanese)
Money 1 new Taiwan dollar = 10 jiao = 100 cent

Japan
Capital City Tokyo
Population 126,804,433
Area 377,915 sq km
Main languages Japanese
Money 1 yen = 100 sen

North Korea
Capital City Pyongyang
Population 22,757,275
Area 120,538 sq km
Main languages Korean
Money 1 won = 100 chon

South Korea
Capital City Seoul
Population 48,636,068
Area 99,720 sq km
Main languages Korean
Money 1 won = 100 jeon

Saudi Arabia
Capital City Riyadh

Population 25,731,776
Area 2,149,690 sq km
Main languages Arabic
Money 1 riyal = 100 halalah

Bahrain
Capital City Manama
Population 738,004
Area 760 sq km
Main languages Arabic
Money 1 Bahraini dinar = 1,000 fils

Pakistan
Capital City Islamabad
Population 184,404,791
Area 796,095 sq km
Main languages English, Urdu, Punjabi, Sindhi, Pashto, Balochi
Money 1 Pakistani rupee = 100 paisa

Nepal
Capital City Kathmandu
Population 28,951,852
Area 147,181 sq km
Main languages Nepali

Money 1 Nepalese rupee = 100 paisa

Myanmar
Capital City Rangoon (Yangon)
Population 53,414,374
Area 676,578 sq km
Main languages Burmese and local languages
Money 1 kyat = 100 pyas

Laos
Capital City Vientiane (Viangchan)
Population 6,368,162
Area 236,800 sq km
Main languages Lao, French
Money 1 new kip = 100 ath

Vietnam
Capital City Hanoi
Population 89,571,130
Area 331,210 sq km
Main languages Vietnamese
Money 1 dong = 100 xu

Qatar
Capital City Doha
Population 840,926
Area 11,586 sq km
Main languages Arabic
Money 1 riyal = 100 dirhams

United Arab Emirates
Capital City Abu Dhabi
Population 4,975,593
Area 83,600 sq km
Main languages Arabic
Money 1 dirham = 100 fils

India
Capital City New Delhi
Population 1,173,108,018
Area 3,287,263 sq km
Main languages Hindi, English and at least 16 other official languages
Money 1 Indian rupee = 100 paise

Bangladesh
Capital City Dhaka
Population 156,118,464
Area 143,998 sq km
Main languages Bengali
Money 1 taka = 100 paisa

Thailand
Capital City Bangkok
Population 67,089,500
Area 513,120 sq km
Main languages Thai
Money 1 baht = 100 satangs

Cambodia
Capital City Phnom Penh
Population 14,453,680
Area 181,035 sq km
Main languages Khmer
Money 1 riel = 100 sen

Brunei
Capital City Bandar Seri
Begawan
Population 395,027
Area 5,765 sq km
Main languages Malay, English,
Chinese
Money 1 Bruneian dollar =
100 cents

Philippines
Capital City Manila
Population 99,900,177
Area 300,000 sq km
Main languages Filipino, English
Money 1 Philippine peso =
100 centavos

Yemen
Capital City Sanaa
Population 23,495,361
Area 527,968 sq km
Main languages Arabic
Money 1 Yemeni riyal = 100 fils

Oman
Capital City Muscat
Population 2,967,717
Area 309,500 sq km
Main languages Arabic
Money 1 rial = 1,000 biaza

Maldives
Capital City Male
Population 395,650
Area 298 sq km
Main languages Divehi
Money 1 rufiyaa = 100 laari

The big, busy port of Singapore

Lots of islands

☆ Singapore is made up of 65 islands. It is one of the smallest countries in the world, and is also known as a 'city-state'. Singapore is one of Asia's busiest ports and it is important for building and repairing ships. It has a huge oil refinery, too.

Sri Lanka
Capital City Colombo
Population 21,513,990
Area 65,610 sq km
Main languages Sinhala, Tamil,
English
Money 1 Sri Lankan rupee =
100 cents

Malaysia
Capital City Kuala Lumpur
Population 28,274,729
Area 329,847 sq km
Main languages Malay, English,
Chinese dialects, Tamil, Telugu,
Malayalam
Money 1 ringgit = 100 sen

Singapore
Capital City Singapore
Population 4,701,069
Area 697 sq km
Main languages English, Malay,
Mandarin, Tamil
Money 1 Singapore dollar =
100 cents

Indonesia
Capital City Jakarta
Population 242,968,342
Area 1,904,569 sq km
Main languages Indonesian and
300 local languages
Money 1 rupiah (*rupiahs are not
divided into smaller units*).

Tea in Sri Lanka

This country is the fourth-biggest tea producer in the world. The tea grows on plantations in the highlands. Then it is sold around the world.

Timor Leste
Capital City Dili
Population 1,154,625
Area 14,874 sq km
Main languages Tetum,
Portuguese, Indonesian,
English
Money 1 US dollar = 100 cents

Australasia and Oceania

The part of the world known as Australasia and Oceania contains 14 countries. The biggest country is Australia, and the smallest is Nauru. Many of the countries here are collections of little islands in the Pacific Ocean. A lot of the tiny islands have their own particular languages and customs. Most of the people here live close to the sea.

Biggest city

The largest city in this region is Sydney, in Australia. This beautiful city is small compared to many of the world's great cities. Only about 4.5 million people live in Sydney.

NORTHERN MARIANA ISLANDS (to US)

GUAM (to US)

MICRONESI

PALAU

PAPUA NEW GUINEA

INDIAN OCEAN

AUSTRALIA

SOUTHERN OCEAN

Biggest country

The biggest country and largest island in this region is Australia. There are big areas of scrubland outside most of the towns and cities. This is called 'the outback'.

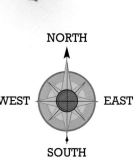

NORTH

WEST — EAST

SOUTH

Smallest country

This is a photo of Nauru, the smallest island that is also a country. Once it was rich from selling guano (bird droppings) to make fertilizer. Now Nauru is poor because most of the guano has been sold.

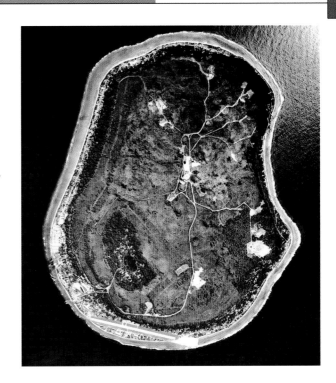

PACIFIC OCEAN

MARSHALL ISLANDS

NAURU

K I R I B A T I

KIRIBATI

TUVALU

TOKELAU
(to NZ)

AMERICAN
SAMOA
(to US)

SOLOMON
ISLANDS

SAMOA

VANUATU

COOK
ISLANDS
(to NZ)

**FRENCH
POLYNESIA
(to France)**

F I J I

TONGA

NIUE
(to NZ)

PITCAIRN
ISLANDS
(to UK)

NEW
CALEDONIA
(to France)

WALLIS &
FUTUNA
(to France)

NEW
ZEALAND

THE WOW!

Australia is one of the oldest islands in the world. It separated from the rest of the land billions of years ago. That is why it has so many unusual plants and animals!

FACTOR

ABOUT AUSTRALASIA AND OCEANIA

NUMBER OF COUNTRIES	14
SIZE	World's 7th-largest continent
TOTAL AREA	9,037,695 sq kilometres
POPULATION	38.9 million people
BIGGEST COUNTRY	Australia – 7,741,220 square kilometres
SMALLEST COUNTRY	Nauru – total area 21 square kilometres
BIGGEST CITY	Sydney, Australia

Australia

Most of Australia is hot, dry desert, known as 'the outback'. It is very difficult to live in a desert, so most of the 20 million people in Australia live close to the coast. It is cooler by the sea and there is more rain, so it is easier to grow crops. Australia is the only country in the world that is also a continent.

1 Koala

This mammal likes eating the leaves of eucalyptus trees, which make the koala feel sleepy!

2 Didgeridoo

This man is playing a didgeridoo. These musical instruments were first made by Aboriginal Australians thousands of years ago. People still play them today. They are often made from eucalpytus wood.

INDIAN OCEAN

KIMBERLEY PLATEAU

GREAT SANDY DESERT

Lake Mackay

GIBSON DESERT

A U

Tropic of Capricorn

WESTERN AUSTRALIA

GREAT VICTORIA DESERT

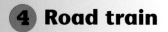

3 Tasmanian devil

This is a mammal that lives on the island of Tasmania. It is as big as a medium-sized dog and it has a very strong bite!

SOUTHERN

4 Road train

Huge trucks called road trains travel thousands of kilometres across the desert. Australia has some of the longest road trains in the world.

Map Labels

Arafura Sea

0 — 200 — 400 kilometres
0 — 200 — 400 miles

ARNHEM LAND ②

Gulf of Carpentaria

CAPE YORK PENINSULA ⑥

Coral Sea

TANAMI DESERT

BARKLY TABLELAND

NORTHERN TERRITORY

GREAT BARRIER REEF ⑤

MACDONNELL RANGES

QUEENSLAND

...TRALIA

▲ Uluru (Ayers Rock) 867m ④

SIMPSON DESERT

SOUTH AUSTRALIA

Lake Eyre North

①

Lake Torrens

Lake Frome

Lake Gairdner

FLINDERS RANGES

Darling River

NEW SOUTH WALES

GREAT DIVIDING RANGE

PACIFIC OCEAN

...CEAN

Murray River

★ **CANBERRA**

Mount Kosciuszko 2228m ▲

VICTORIA AUSTRALIAN ALPS

AUSTRALIAN CAPITAL TERRITORY

Bass Strait

③ **TASMANIA**

Compass
NORTH
WEST — EAST
SOUTH

⑤ Sharks on the reef

The Great Barrier Reef is the world's largest coral reef. This reef is home to many different animals, including sharks, fishes and turtles.

⑥ Saltwater crocodile

The largest reptiles in the world are saltwater crocodiles. They live in northern Australian swamps and rivers.

THE WOW! FACTOR

For 50,000 years before Europeans first settled in Australia, hundreds of different groups of Aboriginal people lived on this land, in harmony with nature.

Pacific Islands

In the Pacific Ocean there are thousands of islands. Many people live here, with lots of different religions and languages. About 200 years ago European people started to move to this area and introduced their own cultures and religions. Most people on these islands are poor and they live by farming and fishing. On some islands tourism is very important.

1 Tree kangaroo

This tree kangaroo lives in the jungles of New Guinea. It is a marsupial, which means that it carries its young in a pouch in its belly. There are nine kinds of tree kangaroo in New Guinea.

2 Maori greeting

The Maori people of New Zealand have special ways of greeting each other. Part of a traditional greeting is pressing their noses together. This is called a 'hongi'.

3 Cyclones

This part of the world has huge storms called cyclones. In a cyclone the wind can blow at up to 120 km an hour. It can destroy buildings and even uproot trees.

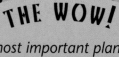

THE WOW! FACTOR

The most important plant in the whole of the Pacific Islands is the coconut palm. It is called 'the tree of life' by local people and every part of it is used or eaten.

Map labels:
Tropic of Cancer
NORTHERN MARIANA ISLANDS (to US)
Mariana
GUAM (to US) ★HAGATNA
OREOR ★
PALAU
MICRONESIA PALIKIR ★
5
Equator
INDONESIA
PAPUA NEW GUINEA
▲ Mount Wilhelm 4509m
1
PORT MORESBY ★
SOL ISL
HONIA
Coral Sea
NE CALEDON (to Fran
AUSTRALIA
Tropic of Capricor

4 Traditional canoes

Many people living on the Pacific Islands still use traditional canoes for travelling and fishing. These canoes are light, fast and stable in rough seas.

5 Stick dance

These people, from one of the islands in the region of Micronesia, are doing a traditional 'stick dance'. They wear colourful costumes and make lots of noise with bamboo sticks!

MIDWAY ISLANDS (to US)

Hawaiian Islands (to US)

Hawaii

NORTH

WEST — EAST

SOUTH

International Date Line

PACIFIC OCEAN

ARSHALL SLANDS

Ratak Chain

Ralik Chain

URU ★ **BAIRIKI**

Equator

KIRIBATI

Line Islands

KIRIBATI

ON OS

TUVALU

★ **FONGAFALE**

Santa Cruz Islands

P *o* *l* *y* *n* *e* *s* *i* *a*

TOKELAU (to New Zealand)

Northern Cook Islands

WALLIS AND FUTUNA (to France)

SAMOA **APIA** ★

AMERICAN SAMOA (to US)

★ **MATA'UTU**

★ **PAGO PAGO**

VANUATU

COOK ISLANDS (to New Zealand)

3 ★ **PAPEETE**

★ **PORT-VILA**

★ **SUVA**

TONGA

NIUE (to New Zealand)

Southern Cook Islands

FRENCH POLYNESIA (to France)

FIJI

★ **ALOFI**

4 ★

NOUMÉA

★ **NUKU'ALOFA**

★ **AVARUA**

7 **PITCAIRN ISLANDS** (to UK)

6 Kiwi

The kiwi is New Zealand's national bird. Kiwis cannot fly, so unfortunately, cats and dogs can catch them easily.

Tasman Sea

2

NEW ZEALAND

★ **WELLINGTON**

6

0   250   500 kilometres

0   250   500 miles

7 Easter Island stones

These ancient stone statues, called Moai, are on a tiny island called Easter Island. There are 887 statues. Most of them have huge heads!

Australasia and Oceania facts

Most of the people here speak English, but there are also thousands of other languages. There are hundreds of religions and cultures too. About half of the countries do not have their own currencies. Instead, they use the US, Australian or New Zealand dollar.

Marshall Islands
Capital City Majuro
Population 65,859
Area 181 sq km
Main languages Marshallese, English
Money 1 US dollar = 100 cents

Palau
Capital City Melekeok
Population 20,879
Area 459 sq km
Main languages Palauan, English
Money 1 US dollar = 100 cents

Micronesia
Capital City Palikir
Population 107,154
Area 702 sq km
Main languages English, Trukese, Pohnpeian, Yapese, Kosrean
Money 1 US dollar = 100 cents

Nauru
Capital City Yaren (unofficial)
Population 9,267
Area 21 sq km
Main languages Nauruan, English
Money 1 Australian dollar = 100 cents

Kiribati
Capital City Tarawa
Population 99,482
Area 811 sq km
Main languages English, Gilbertese
Money 1 Australian dollar = 100 cents

Papua New Guinea
Capital City Port Moresby
Population 6,064,515
Area 462,840 sq km
Main languages English, Tok Pisin, Hiri Motu
Money 1 kina = 100 toea

Solomon Islands
Capital City Honiara
Population 559,198
Area 28,896 sq km
Main languages English, Melanese
Money 1 Solomon Islands dollar = 100 cents

Tuvalu
Capital City Funafuti
Population 10,472
Area 26 sq km
Main languages Tuvaluan, English
Money 1 Tuvaluan dollar, or 1 Australian dollar = 100 cents

Big island

New Guinea is the world's second-biggest island. The country of Papua New Guinea takes up half of this island. There are over 820 languages in Papua New Guinea. A lot of people here live in tribal groups in villages, like their ancestors did hundreds of years ago. These men from Papua New Guinea are wearing traditional headdresses.

Fiji islands

Only a tiny part of the country of Fiji is made up of land. The rest of it is sea. Fiji has over 300 islands and lots of tiny islands called islets. Only about one-third of the islands have people living on them.

Samoa
Capital City Apia
Population 192,001
Area 2,831 sq km
Main languages Samoan, English
Money 1 tala = 100 sene

Fiji
Capital City Suva
Population 875,983
Area 18,274 sq km
Main languages English, Fijian, Hindi
Money 1 Fijian dollar = 100 cents

Australia
Capital City Canberra
Population 21,515,754
Area 7,741,220 sq km
Main languages English
Money 1 Australian dollar = 100 cents

Vanuatu
Capital City Port-Vila
Population 221,552
Area 12,189 sq km
Main languages Bislama, French, English
Money 1 vatu = 100 centimes

Tonga
Capital City Nuku'alofa
Population 122,580
Area 747 sq km
Main languages Tongan, English
Money 1 pa'anga = 100 seniti

New Zealand
Capital City Wellington
Population 4,252,277
Area 267,710 sq km
Main languages English, Maori
Money 1 New Zealand dollar = 100 cents

NEW ZEALAND

★ The beautiful country of New Zealand was one of the last places on Earth to be discovered by humans. A lot of it is still covered in forest. Some of the world's oldest trees, called kauris, still grow here. New Zealand is famous for its sheep farming, wool and leather, and for growing apples and pears, which are exported to Europe.

Sheep grazing on the rich pastures of New Zealand

This carving from New Zealand is called a 'tiki'.

Arctic

The huge area that we call the Arctic is mostly a frozen sea. It is not a country or a continent, but it includes the top parts of Asia, North America and Europe. Not many people live in the Arctic because it is so cold and life here is very hard. The North Pole, at the top of the world, is at the centre of the Arctic.

1 Igloos in the Arctic

In the language of Inuit people 'igloo' is the word for house. Traditional Inuit houses are built out of large blocks of snow.

2 Arctic fox

This little fox has thick fur to keep it warm in the Arctic winters. Every summer its fur changes colour to brown!

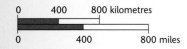

Map labels:
Bering Strait, Arctic Circle, USA (Alaska), Chukchi Sea, RUSSIAN FEDERATION, East Siberian Sea, Limit of summer pack ice, Limit of permanent ice cap, Beaufort Sea, CANADA, Laptev Sea, Victoria Island, ARCTIC OCEAN, Kara Sea, Queen Elizabeth Islands, North Pole, Franz Josef Land, Ellesmere Island, Novaya Zemlya, Baffin Island, Baffin Bay, Wandel Sea, Limit of permanent ice cap, SVALBARD (to Norway), Davis Strait, GREENLAND (to Denmark), Limit of summer pack ice, Limit of winter pack ice, Barents Sea, NUUK, Greenland Sea, Gunnbjørn Fjeld 3,700m, Denmark Strait, NORWAY, FINLAND, Arctic Circle, REYKJAVIK ICELAND

Scale: 0 400 800 kilometres / 0 400 800 miles

3 Polar bear

Polar bears are in danger of extinction. The ice where they hunt for food is melting fast because of global warming.

THE WOW! FACTOR

Earth's temperature is changing. This is making the oceans warmer, so the sea ice has started to melt. By 2030 there may be no ice in the Arctic during the summer months!

Antarctica

This enormous frozen continent is twice the size of the United States of America. It is one of the windiest and coldest places on Earth. Antarctica is a frozen desert and almost all of the land is covered in a thick layer of ice. Nobody lives here all year round because it is too cold, but scientists visit to study the ice and the extreme weather.

1 Ice cliff

This gigantic white cliff is made of solid ice. Sometimes cracks appear in ice cliffs, and huge blocks of ice fall into the sea. The blocks float off as icebergs.

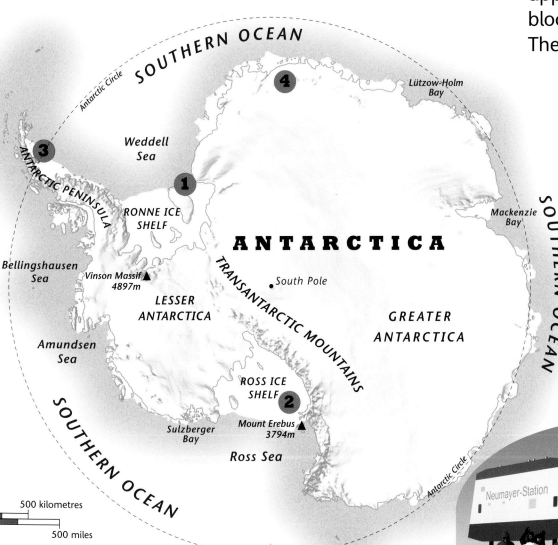

SOUTHERN OCEAN

Antarctic Circle

4

Lützow-Holm Bay

Weddell Sea

ANTARCTIC PENINSULA

3

1

RONNE ICE SHELF

Bellingshausen Sea

Vinson Massif ▲ 4897m

LESSER ANTARCTICA

ANTARCTICA

• South Pole

TRANSANTARCTIC MOUNTAINS

GREATER ANTARCTICA

Mackenzie Bay

SOUTHERN OCEAN

Amundsen Sea

ROSS ICE SHELF

2

Sulzberger Bay

Mount Erebus ▲ 3794m

Ross Sea

SOUTHERN OCEAN

Antarctic Circle

| 0 | 500 kilometres |
| 0 | 500 miles |

2 Emperor penguins

These are the world's tallest penguins. They are 1.2 m tall – about as big as a 6-year-old child.

3 Ice fish

This fish can survive the freezing waters because it has an 'antifreeze' chemical in its blood, which stops it from freezing.

4 Research in Antarctica

This research station is one of about 60 in Antarctica. Scientists study many things here, including the weather, animals and even outer space!

71

Index

The page numbers in **bold** show where the maps are

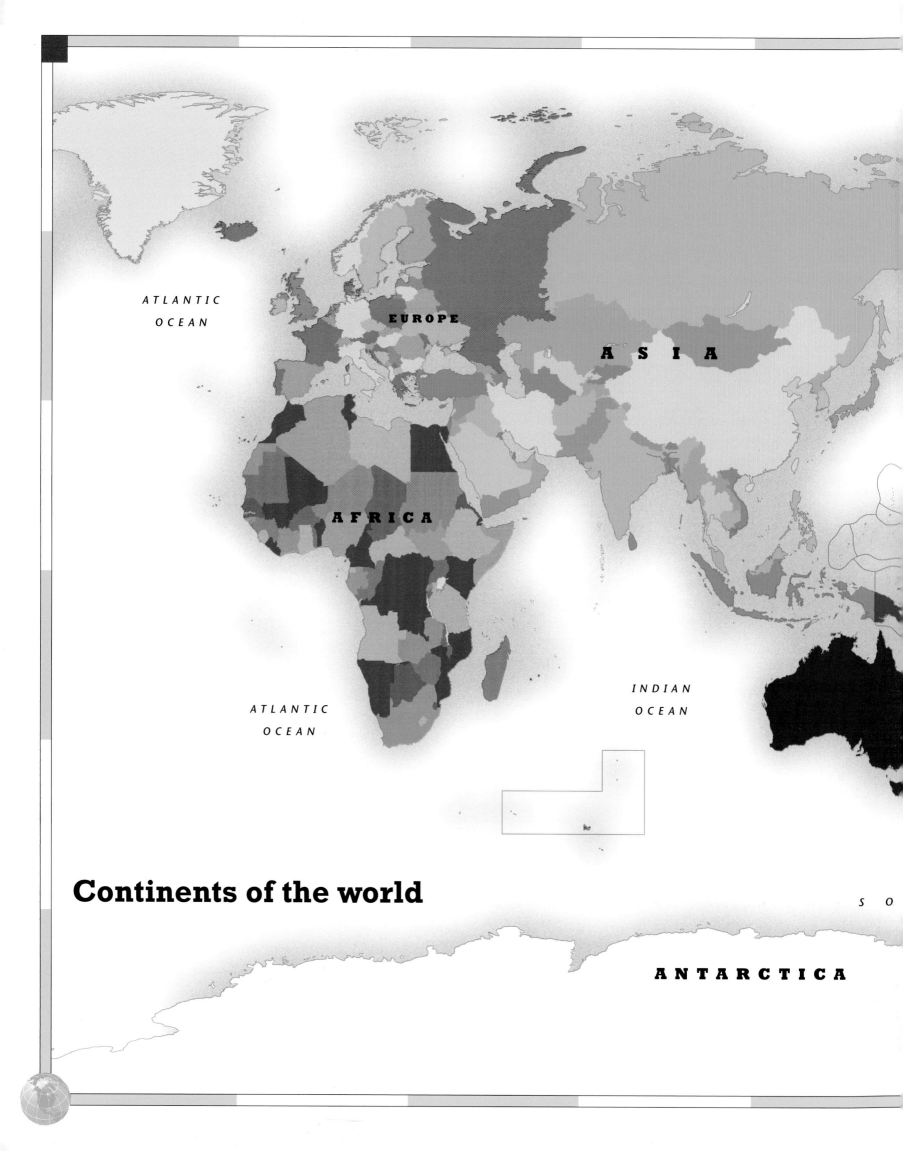

ATLANTIC
OCEAN

EUROPE

ASIA

AFRICA

ATLANTIC
OCEAN

INDIAN
OCEAN

Continents of the world

ANTARCTICA